MORE GAMES

TRAINERS PLAY

EXPERIENTIAL LEARNING EXERCISES

MORE GAMES TRAINERS PLAY

EXPERIENTIAL LEARNING EXERCISES

Edward E. Scannell

Arizona State University

AND

John W. Newstrom

University of Minnesota

McGRAW-HILL BOOK COMPANY

New York   St. Louis   San Francisco   Auckland   Bogotá   Düsseldorf
London   Madrid   Mexico   Montreal   New Delhi   Panama
Paris   São Paulo   Singapore   Sydney   Tokyo   Toronto

Library of Congress Cataloging in Publication Data

Scannell, Edward E.
    More games trainers play

    1. Small groups. 2. Group relations training. 3.   Games.
4. Education games. 5. Education simulation methods.
I. Newstrom, John W. II. Title.

HM133.S3 1983   371.3'07'8   83-5368

ISBN 0-07-055045-X

MORE GAMES TRAINERS PLAY: Experiential Learning Exercises

        6 7 8 9 0 EBEB 8 9 8

The editor was Stephanie Bond; the production supervisor was
Jorge Ramirez; and the design studio was Network Graphics,
Hauppauge, New York.

Edwards Brothers Incorporated was the printer and binder.

This book is dedicated
to those special people
in our lives who have
helped us become better
trainers.

Table Of Contents

Preface

Since <u>Games Trainers Play</u> was published in 1980, there has been an
enthusiastic response to the role of these games in the training process.
This type of widespread interest has encouraged us to prepare a second
set of exercises and to publish it as <u>More Games Trainers Play</u>.

Each year, thousands of people enter the field of Human Resource Development. According to governmental studies, it is the fastest growing profession in America! Because the majority of these people may enter the
field with little training, teaching, or group process experience, their
formal presentation or platform skills may not be as effective as possible.

The purpose in offering <u>More Games</u> is similar to that of its predecessor.
We hope to present a comprehensive sampling of brief training aids designed
to enhance, illustrate, or fortify key points in a session. Most of the
hints and ideas presented were contributed by a large group of training and
development professionals. The exercises have all been field tested, and response indicates successful use for both new and veteran trainers.

Each exercise is presented in a standard format:

> TITLE
> OBJECTIVE
> PROCEDURE
> DISCUSSION QUESTIONS
> MATERIALS REQUIRED
> APPROXIMATE TIME REQUIRED
> SOURCE

For those exercises of an appropriate nature, optional discussion questions
are posed. Typically, these are open-ended questions designed to elicit
discussion, and there are no "right" or "wrong" answers.

We have attempted to research and identify the originator of each activity
in this book. However, many of the exercises have been passed around by
word of mouth, and few documented original sources could be identified.
Therefore, we offer a sincere note of appreciation to everyone who know-
ingly or unknowingly contributed items to this effort.

Finally, we gratefully acknowledge the ready and capable expertise of
Betty Norris and her co-workers, Marty Peck and Francie Sweet, in their
typing and preparation of this work.

Edward E. Scannell
John W. Newstrom

Introduction

DEFINITION
OF GAMES

Professional trainers are responsible for managing the content, process, and environment of a learning situation. Content refers to the facts, data, information, and rules deemed important to ultimate application on the job. Process encompasses the approaches by which that content is delivered. Environment is the physical and psychological surroundings for the training session (location, facilities, arrangements, food, etc.).

This book focuses on games professional trainers and educators can, and do, play. These games are part of the process element of a learning experience. In this book, a game may be an exercise, illustration, activity, or incident used to present or support the trainee's learning. The uniqueness of the game itself will often be sufficient to draw additional attention to the point made and to thereby reinforce it.

Learning, of course, can take place at three levels-- cognitive, affective, or psychomotor. The acquisition of knowledge, attitudes, or skills can be expedited through the selective utilization of an appropriate game.

GAMES VS.
OTHER
EXPERIENTIAL
EXERCISES

Games, as used here, differ from most other experiential exercises such as simulations, board games, computer exercises, role plays, or in-basket exercises. Although it is difficult to generalize, simulations usually attempt to create some significant aspect of a complex organization, and provide an opportunity for realistic implementation of a solution. A range of interrelated factors are often present at both micro and macro levels, and there is often a longitudinal time dimension built into the process. As such, experiential exercises and simulations often require a greater time commitment and are more complex in their setup, operation, and interpretation.

An explanation of the typical characteristics of games will show the marked contrast involved. The point is that games are not advocated here as either better than other approaches or as a replacement for them. Games are different and will be seen as having unique features, making them appropriate for other objectives.

CHARACTERISTICS OF GAMES

Games usually:

1. Are brief. They can range from a one-minute visual illustration or verbal vignette up to a 30-minute group discussion exercise. However, since they are used for supplementing other material, the time devoted to them should be minimized.

2. Are inexpensive. In general, nothing has to be purchased commercially; nor does a consultant need to be engaged. With rare exceptions, the games included here can be used at no cost.

3. Are participative. To be effective, games must involve the trainees physically (through movement) or psychologically (through visual and mental attention). Games draw the trainees' attention, and make them think, react, or laugh.

4. Use props. Several of the games involve the use of a simple prop to add realism to the activity. The prop may be a picture, bag of lemons, sport coat, or deck of cards.

5. Are low-risk. All of the games presented here have been tested many times. If matched to the right context and applied in a positive and professional manner, they will almost always succeed.

6. Are adaptable. The best games, like the best humorous stories, can be adapted to fit any situation and reinforce several different points. They can often be modified slightly and still retain their original flavor and character.

7. Are single-focus. In contrast to simulations, games are often used to illustrate a single point only. As such, they are oriented to micro issues rather than interdependent macro issues.

PROPER USES OF GAMES

An examination of the more than 100 games in this book will reveal that each has a distinctive purpose. They can, however, be classified in various ways according

to their general applications. The major objectives
are:

1. As session icebreakers. Good trainers catch and
    hold the group's attention at the beginning of
    each session. Games are useful devices to "warm
    up" a group, and a pattern of games used like
    this creates further expectations in the minds of
    the trainees.

2. To involve the trainees. Many games require a
    verbal response, physical movement, or intellectual
    activity. Consequently, they invoke the use of
    participation in a positive manner.

3. As illustrations. Extensive presentation of con-
    cepts, theories, and models will bore almost any
    audience. Games can provide vivid examples that
    will be implanted in trainees' memories for longer
    periods of time. In short, a change of pace may
    be just what the doctor ordered.

4. As session closings. In addition to summarizing,
    professional trainers incorporate some device to
    add "zing" to the end of a long hour or day.
    Further, they attempt to stimulate the trainees
    to action. Several of the games are designed to
    facilitate transfer of learning from the training
    context to the work environment.

IMPROPER
USES OF
GAMES

There are many pitfalls in the use of games as a
training tool. Insecure, inexperienced, or unpre-
pared trainers may use games to kill time, to impress
upon trainees how smart they are, or to put down
trainees. When playing the games begins to dominate
the focus of the learning process, most trainees will
perceive the games as being hokey or cute, but dis-
tracting from the overall professionalism of the program. Trainees should be encouraged to ask the questions
of "so what?" or "what's in it for me?" from each game
and should always find at least one answer. Finally,
good games should be neither overly complicated, nor
should they in any way be personally threatening or
demeaning to the participant.

FACILITATION
OF
LEARNING

Several classical principles of learning are incorporated into the use of games. A few of these will

be briefly highlighted here.

1. Repetition: retention of new material or a new skill will be increased if the trainee hears it more than once or practices a new behavior several times. Insertion of a game into a training module allows the trainer to reiterate a point in another fashion and thereby increase the probability of retention and application.

2. Reinforcement: many of the games described in this book provide an opportunity for success or achievement on the part of the participants. By providing pleasant consequences for their behavior, that behavior is reinforced and consequently is more likely to be repeated in the future.

3. Association: much of our learning is not totally new, but is tangential to what is already known. In other words, it is often easier for us to move gradually from a base of knowledge to the unknown. Games--even familiar ones--help us make the kind of connections between different contexts that ease the process of learning. Later on, the trainee may first recall the game, but then can make an easy transition to the underlying principle.

4. Senses: researchers tell us that learning is more effective when increasing numbers of the five basic senses are involved (sight, sound, smell, taste, and touch). Games generally build upon all but smell, and thereby add a second or third dimension to the classical learning process.

NEW AND
DIFFERENT
GAMES

The games contained in this book represent only a small sample of those popularly used in education and training today. Readers are encouraged to screen these games, pilot-test them to determine their own comfort level, and then use selected games to provide a refreshing change of pace to their programs. A second suggestion is to become an astute observer of other trainers and speakers, thereby acquiring an expanded set of trainer's games. A third recommendation is to develop your own set of games. This process should begin with clear answers to the questions of "What are my goals? How much time do I have? Who will be participating? What point am I trying to illustrate? How will my trainees respond?"

CONCLUSION   Training is a very serious business. Looked upon as
                  the core of a training program, trainer's games are
                  doomed to mockery and failure. When viewed as useful
                  supplements to be used occasionally to reinforce and
                  strengthen learning, games assume their rightful posi-
                  tion in a subordinate role. Trainers who are willing
                  to experiment with some new tools to enhance personal
                  effectiveness should benefit greatly from these games.

I.

CLIMATE

SETTING AND

ICEBREAKERS

Name Tag Mixer

OBJECTIVE: To be used as an initial get-acquainted exercise.

PROCEDURE: As each participant enters the meeting room, check
               off his/her name on the roster, but present a
               different person's name tag. Explain that they
               should seek one another out, and also introduce
               themselves to other participants as well. If the
               group is relatively small (up to 30-35 participants),
               have the paired individuals interview each other so
               they can introduce their counterparts to the rest of
               the group.

MATERIALS
REQUIRED: Name tags.

APPROXIMATE
TIME
REQUIRED: Fifteen-twenty minutes.

SOURCE: Unknown.

What's Your Name?

OBJECTIVE: To let new participants become acquainted with several
                       of their colleagues in a fun and informal way.

PROCEDURE: Divide the participants into groups of six-eight
                       people. Ask them to stand, forming a circle for
                       each separate group. Each group is given a whiffle
                       ball (or similar soft object) and as it is tossed
                       from one person to another, the receiver simply calls
                       out his/her first name and throws it to another in
                       that circle. Continue the process for three-four
                       minutes or until you feel each person knows the names
                       of the other people in that group.

MATERIALS
REQUIRED: A soft ball for each group.

APPROXIMATE
TIME
REQUIRED: Five-ten minutes.

SOURCE: Wayne Shannon, Nashville, Tennessee.

Word Games

OBJECTIVE: To "mark-time" at the beginning of a session, i.e.,
              you want to start the session at the announced time,
              but only a portion of the audience is in attendance.

PROCEDURE: Only those in the room at the announced time (i.e.,
              8 a.m., 1:15 p.m., etc.) are given the form shown on
              the following page. Individuals are asked to work on
              their own although latecomers may assist if they want.
              (Typically, those arriving after the announced time
              get the message that you intend to stay on schedule.)

MATERIALS
REQUIRED: Form as shown.

APPROXIMATE
TIME
REQUIRED: Five-ten minutes maximum.

SOURCE: Contributed by Dr. Ralph C. Hook, University of Hawaii,
              Honolulu, Hawaii.

This test does not measure your intelligence, your fluency with words, and certainly not your mathematical ability. It will, however, give you some gauge of your mental flexibility and creativity.

Examine each of the following and identify what each acronym, phrase or abbreviation shows.

1.   26 = L of the A   ****Sample****   26 = Letters of the Alphabet.

2.   7 = W of the A W _____

3.   1,001 = A N _____

4.   12 = S of the Z_____

5.   54 = C in a D (with the J's)_____

6.   9 = P in the S S _____

7.   88 = P K_____

8.   13 = S on the A F_____

9.   32 = D F at which W F_____

10. 18 = H on a G C_____

11. 90 = D in a R A_____

12. 200 = D for P G in M_____

13.   8 = S on a S S_____

14.   3 = B M (SHTR)_____

15.   4 = Q in a G_____

16. 24 = H in a D_____

17.   1 = W on a U_____

18.   5 = D in a Z C_____

19. 57 = H V_____

20. 11 = P on a F T_____

21. 1,000 = W that a P is W_____

22. 29 = D in F in a L Y_____

23. 64 = S on a C_____

24. 40 = D and N of the G F_____

Answers to the Word Games

1. 26 Letters of the Alphabet
2. 7 Wonders of the Ancient World
3. 1,001 Arabian Nights
4. 12 Signs of the Zodiac
5. 54 Cards in a Deck
6. 9 Planets in the Solar System
7. 88 Piano Keys
8. 13 Stripes on the American Flag
9. 32 Degrees F. at which Water Freezes
10. 18 Holes on a Golf Course
11. 90 Degrees in a Right Angle
12. 200 Dollars for Passing Go in Monopoly
13. 8 Sides on a Stop Sign
14. 3 Blind Mice (See How They Run)
15. 4 Quarts in a Gallon
16. 24 Hours in a Day
17. 1 Wheel on a Unicycle
18. 5 Digits in a Zip Code
19. 57 Heinz Variety
20. 11 Players on a Football Team
21. 1,000 Words that a Picture is Worth
22. 29 Days in February in a Leap Year
23. 64 Squares on a Checkerboard
24. 40 Days and Nights of the Great Flood

Nonverbal Walk

OBJECTIVE:
To illustrate the impact of nonverbal communication and to recognize the importance of stereotypes and first impressions.

PROCEDURE:
As an icebreaker before anyone has had an opportunity to be verbally introduced, conduct a nonverbal walk. For approximately five minutes, have the group walk around the room observing other participants without speaking. They may use gestures, eye contact or other facial expressions (smiles, winks, frowns, etc.), but they may not talk.

They should develop, either mentally or on paper, five impressions of each of the persons they observe. When the five minutes are up, form groups of five-seven to discuss the first impressions and to allow for any corrections of misperceptions. When impressions are shared with all the members observed within one group, they may move to another small group and share impressions with them.

If time allows, when individuals have shared with everyone in the small group setting, regroup and discuss the exercise.

DISCUSSION
QUESTIONS:

1. Were most first impressions accurate? Why? Why not?

2. Were any accurate clues given nonverbally? Facial expressions? Clothes? Hair style? Posture?

3. Did you find it difficult not to talk? Why? Why not?

4. Would you have been more comfortable if allowed to talk?

MATERIALS
REQUIRED:
Paper and pencil (optional).

APPROXIMATE
TIME
REQUIRED:
Twenty-thirty minutes.

SOURCE:
Jacqueline V. Markus, Department of Communication, Arizona State University, Tempe, Arizona.

What's My Line?

OBJECTIVE: To illustrate the importance of first impressions and stereotyping.

PROCEDURE: This is a variation of the self introduction game, using name, job and favorite hobby. Instead of introductions that way, individuals are asked to introduce the person on their right. However, this is done strictly by guess-work, i.e., no clues are exchanged.

After a brief observation of the person on the right, introduce him/her with a name (first only), job, and favorite hobby that you "think" he/she has, giving brief reasons for your guesses.

The person being guessed will then respond with the correct information before proceeding on with his/her introduction. Continue around the circle until everyone has been introduced. (If you have done the first part of this exercise in a small group, now return to a large group setting, positioning yourself so that the same person is still on your right. You will then introduce the person on your right to the larger group.)

DISCUSSION QUESTIONS:

1. How accurate are first impressions?

2. What do we base them on?

3. Have you ever opted not to meet someone, based on your first impressions?

4. What are stereotypes? Why do we make them?

5. Do you now feel more comfortable with this group than when you arrived?

6. Do you know more about the people here than when you first arrived?

MATERIALS REQUIRED: None.

APPROXIMATE TIME REQUIRED: Twenty-thirty minutes.

SOURCE: Jacqueline V. Markus, Department of Communication, Arizona State University, Tempe, Arizona.

Expectations

OBJECTIVE: To be used at the very start of a training program or session in order to allow individuals a chance to express their personal feelings and expectations on the outcomes of the program.

PROCEDURE: Display or distribute copies of the "Expectations" questions to the group. Ask each person to write out his/her response to each question. Give an example or two to set the group at ease.

EXPECTATIONS

1. What do I see as personal goals for this session?

2. What could I do if these personal goals are not met?

3. What are some things I hope will not happen in this session?

4. What are my feelings right now about this experience?

After a few minutes of this, ask participants to move about the room and form groups of two-three people and discuss their responses. After ten-twelve minutes, re-assemble group and ask for a few sample group reports.

Cautionary Note: Be prepared to respond if attendees' expectations differ markedly from the session objectives. If possible, some alteration or change may be reached as a compromise if the majority of the group so suggests.

MATERIALS
REQUIRED: Handout sheets (optional).

APPROXIMATE
TIME
REQUIRED: Twenty-thirty minutes.

SOURCE: Unknown.

Magic Circle

OBJECTIVE:

To serve as an icebreaker and to illustrate the multiplicity of meanings of words.

PROCEDURE:

Divide the group into teams of five-seven people. If possible, arrange the chairs in a circular fashion. On a prepared set of 3"x 5"cards, a series of words or phrases are written (one on each card, e.g., motivation; put-down; I feel good when...). The group leader pulls a card at random and each person is asked to state what the word means to them, or in the case of sentence completion, continue the statement. Continue for five-seven minutes for each card.

DISCUSSION QUESTIONS:

1. What barriers to effective communication did the exercise show?

2. Misinterpretations and misunderstandings often occur in communication. How can we use this activity to help reduce these errors?

3. Words have many meanings. How can we help ensure that senders and receivers get on the same wave length?

MATERIALS REQUIRED:

3" x 5" cards with words printed.

APPROXIMATE TIME REQUIRED:

Fifteen-twenty minutes.

SOURCE:

Unknown.

Siblings

OBJECTIVE: To serve as an initial get-acquainted icebreaker.

PROCEDURE: Before the content session begins, ask the group to divide themselves in the four corners of the room with these subsets:

1. If they were the oldest in the family,

2. If they were the youngest in the family,

3. If they were any place in the middle,

4. If they were an only child.

As the participants seek out their respective groups, ask them to recall what they liked or disliked about their respective places in their growing up days. For example, the oldest may have had to care for their younger brother(s) or sister(s) or the youngest may have had all the "hand-me-down" clothes. In retrospect, would they have preferred a different place?

After each group has ten-fifteen minutes to discuss these and other questions, ask for one person to respond for each group. (Groups should be limited to eight-ten people.)

MATERIALS
REQUIRED: None.

APPROXIMATE
TIME
REQUIRED: Twenty minutes.

SOURCE: Unknown.

Giving Away Secrets

OBJECTIVE: To use a quick demonstration to attract and focus the group's attention on you and the presentation to follow.

PROCEDURE: Give each participant a piece of blank paper. Explain that they are going to know the person sitting next to them through an arithmetic exercise. Have each person:

1. Write the numerical part of their address on the blank paper;

2. Multiply the address by 2;

3. Add 5;

4. Multiply by 50;

5. Add their age;

6. Add 365;

7. Have each participant pick a partner and share only the total of this exercise with them.

Example: 3202   (Address)
            x2   (Multiply)
           ─────
            6404
            +5   (Add)
           ─────
            6409
            x50   (Multiply)
          ───────
           320450
           +45   (Add)
          ───────
           320495
           +365   (Add)
          ───────
           320860   (Total Given to Partner)

After each has shown the number, have them subtract 615. The resulting total will give you the age (the last two numbers) and the address of the individual.

Example
Continued: 320860   (Total Given to Partner)
              -615   (Subtracted by Partner)
             ───────
              320245

              Address: 3202   Age: 45

Explain that they have just shared with their partner their address and age.

MATERIALS
REQUIRED: Blank paper and pencils or pens.

APPROXIMATE
TIME
REQUIRED: Five minutes.

SOURCE: Unknown. Used by Richard A. Robinson, Jr., State of
                     Washington.

What's Your Sign?

OBJECTIVE:
To be used as an initial icebreaker and as a get-acquainted exercise.

PROCEDURE:
At the beginning of a session where participants are not acquainted with their fellow attendees, this exercise will ease introductions. Ask people to shout out their astrological signs and then group themselves accordingly. (For those who don't know what sign they are, have them state their birthdates and someone in the group will assist them in identifying it.) Have each of the groups physically move to a part of the room where they can introduce themselves and discuss some of the readily associated traits with their respective signs. (If working with larger groups, limit the sub-groups to 8-10 participants.) If time permits, ask a few groups to report their findings.

DISCUSSION QUESTIONS:

1. Are the traits and characteristics of your sign valid ones?

2. Do we sometimes let our "signs" influence our behavior? Why or why not?

3. Have you seen cases when one's astrological sign has been helpful (or obstructive) in work relationships?

4. Do your own self-perceptions "fit" your sign?

MATERIALS REQUIRED:
None.

APPROXIMATE TIME REQUIRED:
Ten-fifteen minutes.

SOURCE:
Unknown.

Who Am I?

OBJECTIVE: To provide a novel method for getting acquainted.

PROCEDURE:

1. Explain to the group that the objective of the exercise is to allow them to get acquainted with each other by expressing themselves through an object of their choice.

2. Tell them that they each have 15 minutes to search the surrounding area (inside and outside, if appropriate) to find something that they feel represents some of their characteristics or expresses who they are. Ask them to bring it to the seminar room.

3. Call on each participant to show what he/she selected and explain what it represents (e.g., "I picked a rock because it is strong, smooth, colorful, and old.")

DISCUSSION QUESTIONS:

1. What did you learn about the other participants?

2. What reaction do you have to the variety of objects chosen to express their character?

3. To what degree do you feel that you now know the other participants better?

MATERIALS REQUIRED: None

APPROXIMATE TIME REQUIRED: Thirty minutes, but it depends on group size.

SOURCE: Beverly Wright, Greyhound Corporation, Phoenix, Arizona.

Handful Of Icebreakers

OBJECTIVE: To help participants become acquainted with, and feel comfortable about, each other early in a session.

PROCEDURE:

1. Pair up the participants. Instruct them to interview each other on the basis of:

   a. Three unusual things that have happened in their lives.

   b. Special talents or hobbies they have.

   c. The two most important job responsibilities that they have.

   d. The person that they most admire (or despise) in the world.

   e. A color and an animal that best describe who they are and how they feel.

2. Ask the group to introduce themselves as they think their best friend would--their likes and dislikes, recreational interests, personal aspirations, etc.

3. Ask the group to examine and describe what is in their name. They should tell their full name, any nickname or abbreviation, who they were named after, and whether they like or dislike their name. Also, they should tell what other name they would choose if they had the opportunity (and why).

4. Procure a soft ball (tennis ball or sponge-construction ball). Arrange the participants in a circle. Throw the ball to one person and ask that individual to disclose something unusual about him/her. Then have the ball thrown to another and repeat the process. Only upon the second receipt of the ball should they disclose their first names.

5. Prior to the session, survey (by phone or letter) the participants to discover various information such as their hobbies, job title, major accomplishments, self-descriptive adjectives, etc. Then prepare a brief synopsis of each (with name deleted) and distribute to the group at the beginning of the session. After the first coffee break, invite everyone to fill in the names that they believe match the descriptions. Provide the "key" to help them complete the form.

MATERIALS
REQUIRED: Ball (for #4), or form (for #5).

APPROXIMATE
TIME
REQUIRED: Various, depending on the alternative chosen.

SOURCES: Faith Galbraith, Genesco; C. Stone, Camp Fire;
                           S. H. Zutler, Dow Chemical; Jon Harris, Naval Underwater
                           Systems Center; Mike Rabalais, Hinds Junior College;
                           Neal Jensen, Edwards Lab; Sue Gatton, Ft. Worth National
                           Bank; and Richard Graheim, Armco.

List The Ways

OBJECTIVE: To immediately stimulate interest in the subject to be discussed.

PROCEDURE: To open a session on any subject (e.g., Managing Time), ask each person in the group to name one way that a supervisor can either lose or waste time. Go around the room quickly, record each person's contribution on a flip chart, and don't allow any criticism or discussion until everyone has participated. The benefits are that people become immediately involved and the list creates interest in the subject as well as a motivation to learn.

DISCUSSION QUESTIONS:

1. Create a list of the positive principles that supervisors can use to save time.

2. Create a list of the proscriptions (things supervisors should avoid) that will also save time.

MATERIALS REQUIRED: Flip chart, pad and pen.

APPROXIMATE TIME REQUIRED: Ten-fifteen minutes

SOURCE: Eugene C. Fetteroll, Jr., Associated Industries of Massachusetts, Boston, Massachusetts.

The New Millionaire

OBJECTIVES:
1. To stimulate trainees to stretch their minds.
2. To create an atmosphere in which sharing is accepted and encouraged.

PROCEDURE:
Assemble the group (standing or sitting) in a circle. Inform them that they have now each been given a gift of one million dollars, tax-free. Ask them to indicate to the group how they would use their newly-gained fortune.

Select one person to start the discussion and then rotate around the room. A contrasting method is to ask for a volunteer to begin, and then let all others contribute their fantasy whenever they feel comfortable doing so.

ALTERNATE PROCEDURE:
Instead of the gift of money, you might ask:

1. If you could take a free two-week trip to any place in the world, where would it be?
2. If you could become the leader of any country in the world, what would it be and why?
3. If you could travel on a time machine to any era in time, what would it be and why?
4. If you could talk to any one person now living, who would it be?

DISCUSSION QUESTIONS:
1. What did you learn about the other persons in this group?
2. In what ways can you use the concept underlying this exercise to help you be more open to new ideas from this training program?

MATERIALS REQUIRED:
Flip chart, if you wish to record the responses.

APPROXIMATE TIME REQUIRED:
One minute per participant.

SOURCE:
Noble Morrell, Department of Human Resources, Topeka, Kansas.

Beyond Murphy

OBJECTIVE: To be used as a change of pace or as a "breather" when everything seems to be going wrong.

PROCEDURE: Explain that the beginning of Murphy's Law (Whatever can go wrong--will) is attributed to an Air Force captain who apparently created the now-famous phrase when a series of errors and problems kept appearing in a California Air Force base missile site. These are some follow-up items to which most people can relate.

1. Left to themselves, things tend to go from bad to worse.

2. Whenever you set out to do something, something else must be done first.

3. Nothing is as easy as it looks.

4. Everything takes longer than you think.

5. If there is a possibility of several things going wrong, the one that will cause the most damage will be the one.

6. Nature always sides with the hidden flaw.

7. It always costs more than first estimated.

8. It is easier to get involved in something than to get out of it.

9. Every solution breeds new problems.

10. If you try to please everybody, somebody will be disappointed.

11. It is impossible to make anything foolproof, because fools are so clever.

12. If you tinker with anything long enough it will break.

13. By making things absolutely clear, people will become confused.

14. If there is a 50 per cent chance of success, that means there is a 75 per cent chance of failure.

15. Interchangeable parts won't.

16. In any computation, the figure that is OBVIOUSLY correct will be the source of error.

17. Blame will never be placed if enough people are involved.

18. Nothing is lost until you begin to look for it.

19. If in the course of several months only three worthwhile social events take place, they will all fall on the same evening.

20. "Murphy was an optimist!"

MATERIALS
REQUIRED: None.

APPROXIMATE
TIME
REQUIRED: Three-five minutes.

SOURCE: Adopted from Laurence J. Peter, author of the Peter Principle.

Fun With States

PURPOSE:

To be used as a warm-up activity or as a "fun" way to reopen a training session after a lunch or coffee break.

PROCEDURE:

Reproduce the quiz section and hand out to participants. The answers are on the next page.

1. Anagrammatically speaking, there are seven states hidden in these word groups. Rearrange the letters to find them:

   a. Ah! Look ma.

   b. I own gym.

   c. Men, share whip.

   d. Loan torn chair.

   e. Horned dials.

   f. Coins wins.

   g. Show inn tag.

2. Name state capitals that begin with "A".

3. How many of these can you answer without an atlas or a dictionary?

   a. Name the only U. S. state that starts and ends with the same letter, other than "A".

   b. "Florida" starts with two consonants. Name another such state.

   c. The name of one state is made up of a common word and its opposite, separated by a single letter. Which state?

   d. If you drop the first and last letters from "Nevada", you're left with the common first name DAVE, spelled backward. What state, without its first and last letters, is a popular actor's <u>last</u> name, spelled backward?

   e. Two different words meaning "employ" are hidden in the names of two states. Which states?

   f. Which state ends with a five-letter women's name? Which one has a man's nickname spelled backward inside a woman's name?

MATERIALS
REQUIRED: Copies of questions.

APPROXIMATE
TIME
REQUIRED: Ten minutes.

SOURCE: Unknown.

ANSWERS:

1. a. Oklahoma
   b. Wyoming
   c. New Hampshire
   d. North Carolina
   e. Rhode Island
   f. Wisconsin
   g. Washington

2. Albany, New York
   Annapolis, Maryland
   Atlanta, Georgia
   Augusta, Maine
   Austin, Texas

3. a. Ohio
   b. Rhode Island
   c. Connecticut
   d. Wyoming, Nimoy (Mr. Spock of "Star Trek")
   e. Massachusetts (use) and New Hampshire (hire)
   f. Indiana (Diana); Montana (Nat spelled backward inside Mona)

People Bingo

OBJECTIVE: To assist participants in getting acquainted with other attendees. This is best used in groups of twenty-five or more.

PROCEDURE: As each person enters the room, they are given a 3" x 5" card with a number that coincides with bingo cards (e.g., B-12, G-51, 0-72, etc.). They are also given regular bingo cards on which they are asked to seek out others who then sign their name under the respective letter heading (example: B-7, Jerry Smith).

When twenty-four names are filled in the proper boxes, the individual signs his/her card and brings it to the registration table. Prizes could be awarded to the first person completing the task.

MATERIALS
REQUIRED: 3" x 5" cards, bingo cards, prizes (optional).

APPROXIMATE
TIME
REQUIRED: Fifteen minutes.

SOURCE: Varied.

Jigsaw Puzzle

OBJECTIVE: To be used as an informal way to be initially introduced to several other participants.

PROCEDURE: Obtain several children's puzzles (six-eight pieces) or cut up company logos or pictures. As each person enters the room, randomly distribute to each a piece of the puzzle. Individuals are then asked to search out the remaining parts of the picture or puzzle and get acquainted. Prizes may be awarded to the first team who completes the task. (If this exercise precedes a meal function, have attendees seated together at tables.)

MATERIALS
REQUIRED: Logos, pictures or children's puzzles.

APPROXIMATE
TIME
REQUIRED: Ten-fifteen minutes.

SOURCE: Unknown.

Meeting New Friends

OBJECTIVE: To serve as an initial get-acquainted exercise.

PROCEDURE: Prepare, in advance, a sheet similar to the one on
                       the following page. (If you are not well acquainted
                       with your attendees, a phone call in advance or a
                       conversation with a colleague should secure the
                       necessary information for you.) Hand each person
                       the form as they walk in to the opening session.

MATERIALS
REQUIRED: Form similar to illustration to hand out.

APPROXIMATE
TIME
REQUIRED: Ten-fifteen minutes, dependent on size of group.

SOURCE: Joel Weldon & Associates, Scottsdale, Arizona.

WELDONS' WHOOSITS

ILLUSTRATION:

1. WHO brought the Weldons to Arizona?_____

2. WHO invited Joel to his first Toastmasters meeting in 1969?_____

3. WHO bought the first set of Earl Nightingale's complete library from Joel in 1972?_____

4. WHO was the first to hire Joel for a paid speaking engagement?_____

5. WHO was the first to hire Joel to speak more than once?_____

6. WHO handled the production work on Joel's first audio cassettes?_____

7. WHO has given the Weldons over five years of one-day printing service, including pick-up and delivery?

   _____

8. WHO has handled Joel's airline tickets for almost five years?_____

9. WHO introduces Joel on his Creative Prospecting cassette album?_____

10. WHO transcribed Joel's audio cassettes at 120 wpm?

   _____

11. WHO helped the Weldons stash away 40% of their income in a pension plan?_____

12. WHO is the studio engineer who cleans up Joel's tapes?

   _____

13. WHO handles production of the "You Can" cassette programs?_____

14. WHO does the Weldons' taxes and accounting? _____
   _____and_____

15. WHO typed the scripts for "Sell It With the Million Dollar Attitude"?_____

16. WHO is the Weldons' corporate attorney?_____

17. WHO does all the Weldons' fine two-color printing?

   _____

18. WHO handles the Weldons' general insurance and settles claims FAST?_____

19. WHO takes care of the Weldons' office supply needs?

   _____

20. WHO is the "Corporate Mother"?_____

Get-Acquainted Scavenger Hunt

OBJECTIVE: To serve as an initial get-acquainted exercise for
                     a group that is attending a two-three day program.

PROCEDURE: Prepare a form similar to the one on the next page.
                     Change the items to tailor it to your respective
                     firm or organization. After the opening welcome,
                     hand out the forms and ask each person to walk
                     around, introduce him or herself and determine what
                     item might fit. Each person can sign on only one
                     line, thereby encouraging more involvement and
                     movement. Announce that the first completed form
                     turned in will get a prize.

MATERIALS
REQUIRED: Form as shown; an inexpensive prize.

APPROXIMATE
TIME
REQUIRED: Ten-fifteen minutes.

SOURCE: Lois Hedlund, Arizona Credit Union League, Phoenix,
                     Arizona.

SAMPLE SCAVENGER HUNT

This Scavenger Hunt should help you break the ice with others attending the meeting. Find a person who answers the question. Have the person sign his or her name. One person can sign only once--so you have to find ten people. The first six people to complete the form win a prize.

1. Find a person who has the same ZODIAC SIGN
    as yours:_____

2. Find a person born EAST OF THE MISSISSIPPI
    RIVER:_____

3. Find a person who has lived in ARIZONA MORE
    THAN 10 YEARS:_____

4. Find a person who is a BUSINESS MANAGER OF A
    COMPANY:_____

5. Find a person who has worked for a company
    OVER 5 YEARS:_____

6. Find a person who belongs to a CREDIT UNION:_____

7. Find a person from a UNIVERSITY:_____

8. Find a person from a COMMUNITY COLLEGE:_____

9. Find a person who has attended a TRAINING
    PROGRAM:_____

10. HOW MANY ONES ARE THERE ON A ONE DOLLAR BILL:_____

II.

LEARNING

Relearning To Count

OBJECTIVE: To impress upon trainers, supervisors, etc. the importance of presenting new material to trainees in an organized manner so as to maximize the efficiency of the learning process.

PROCEDURE:

1. Inform trainees that they are about to learn a totally new symbolic system for counting that will replace the traditional numeric system (1-10).

2. Divide the class into two groups, and provide each group with a different set of instructions.

3. Provide group A with a sheet of paper on which are printed the ten codes for numbers 1-10, and tell them that they have a very limited time to memorize the new system.

4. Provide group B with a sheet of paper on which the codes for numbers 1-10 are shown in conjunction with the spatial figure from which they are drawn (plus X=10). Tell them that they have a very limited time to memorize the new system.

5. Provide two minutes to each group to learn their system, then administer a brief quiz by asking them to write down the codes for a set of numbers that you read off.

DISCUSSION QUESTIONS:

1. Which group scored the highest? Why?

2. What implications does this demonstration of rote vs. concept learning, or unpatterned vs. systematic learning, have for you in your job?

MATERIALS REQUIRED: Preprinted sets of instructions.

APPROXIMATE TIME REQUIRED: Ten-fifteen minutes.

SOURCE: C. Spetz, ACCO, Houston, Texas.

RELEARNING TO COUNT

INSTRUCTIONS: GROUP A: 1 = ⌐

2 = ⊔

3 = ∟

4 = ⊐

5 = ▢

6 = ⊏

7 = ⌐|

8 = ⊓

9 = Γ

10 = X

GROUP B:

1	2	3
4	5	6
7	8	9

1	2	3
4	5	6
7	8	9

10 = X

Reflection Time

OBJECTIVE: To encourage participants to use an overlooked learning style.

PROCEDURE: Instructors should pause periodically (especially following the introduction of new material) and direct the trainees to spend the next one-two minutes quietly reflecting on what they recently heard or experienced. During this silent time, participants should:

1. Mentally summarize the highlights of the last module.

2. Search for applications in their own jobs.

3. Generate questions to direct back to the speaker.

Prior to the spontaneous usage of this approach, participants should be briefed on the nature and value of reflection as a learning style. Further, they may fruitfully be directed toward a descriptive source of material on the topic, such as that by Kolb, Rubin, and McIntyre in ORGANIZATIONAL PSYCHOLOGY: AN EXPERIENTIAL APPROACH, published by Prentice-Hall, Inc.

DISCUSSION
QUESTIONS:

1. What major insights did you develop during the process of reflection?

2. In what ways will you apply your new knowledge to the job?

3. What questions are running through your mind?

MATERIALS
REQUIRED: None.

APPROXIMATE
TIME
REQUIRED: Two minutes for each iteration.

SOURCE: F. E. (Gene) Young, Bureau of Financial Institutions, Richmond, Virginia.

Disvoweled Terminology

OBJECTIVES:

1. To expedite trainee learning and retention of important vocabulary terms.

2. To remove the stigma of testing from the process of evaluation.

PROCEDURE:

Select the most important terms and concepts that will be (have been) presented in a training module. Remove the vowels and punctuation from each word or phrase, leaving only the consonants with no spaces in between. Create a worksheet for distribution to each participant, as shown on the following page. Provide each trainee with a copy, instructing him or her to identify the relevant term from the course material.

ALTERNATE
PROCEDURES:

1. Provide the worksheet to the participants in advance of your presentation, so that they may use the anticipatory process to further add to their learning.

2. Offer some nominal prize or provide recognition to those who score the highest or finish first with all items correct, as an incentive for increasing their motivation.

3. If you wish to speed up the process further, let the participants work in small groups while completing the exercise.

DISCUSSION
QUESTIONS:

1. What was your reaction to this method of evaluation?

2. Did receiving the items in advance help or hinder your learning them?

MATERIALS
REQUIRED:

One worksheet for each participant.

APPROXIMATE
TIME
REQUIRED:

Variable, depending on number and complexity of items, and format chosen (individual or group).

SOURCE:

Adapted from exercise created by Doug and Jan Heller and the staff of "Games" magazine.

DISVOWELED TERMINOLOGY: ILLUSTRATIONS

Disvoweled Term	Key
TRAINING TERMS	
1. NDS	Needs
2. VLTN	Evaluation
3. BJCTVS	Objectives
4. PRTST	Pretest
5. LRNNG	Learning
MOVIE TITLES	
1. DLVRNC	Deliverance
2. STRWRS	Star Wars
3. DRN	Dr. No
4. STRSBRN	A Star Is Born
5. TRGRT	True Grit
ORGANIZATIONAL TITLES	
1. FRMN	Foreman
2. CHRMNFTIIBRD	Chairman of the Board
3. MNGMNTTRN	Management Trainee
4. SPRVSR	Supervisor
5. SCRTRY	Secretary
AMERICAN PRESIDENTS	
1. NXN	Nixon
2. DMS	Adams
3. SNHWR	Eisenhower
4. CLDG	Coolidge
5. MNR	Monroe

Practice Makes Perfect

OBJECTIVES:

1. To demonstrate to participants that repeated practice of a motor skill results in marked improvement.

2. To illustrate vividly to trainees that they must be alert to multiple stimuli in their work environments, and be able to respond quickly to them.

PROCEDURE:

Form the group into pairs. Provide each pair with one copy of the figure on the next page. Assign the role of operator to one person and observer to the other for the first round. Instruct the operators to touch each square in format A in numerical order as fast as they can, while the observer times them. Repeat the process four additional times.

Now have the operator move to format B and measure their success on that set of numbers five times. Then move on to format C, and repeat it five times in total. If time permits, the operator and observer may then switch roles and repeat the entire procedure.

DISCUSSION
QUESTIONS:

1. What happened to the operator's performance times between formats A, B, and C? (It should have sharply increased.)

2. What happened to the operator's performance times across the five iterations of each format? (It should have improved in most cases, at least on the more complex layouts.)

3. How many different actions or distractions compete for your attention on the job? Are you capable of screening these conditions, prioritizing them, and acting accordingly, all in split-second sequence? If not, can you now see the value of repeated practice?

MATERIALS
REQUIRED:

Duplicated copies of the practice sets.

APPROXIMATE
TIME
REQUIRED:

Fifteen minutes.

SOURCE:

Adapted from comments by Mary E. Cobarruvias on safe driving under emergency conditions.

PRACTICE SETS

A.

4	2
1	3

PERIOD	TIME
1	___
2	___
3	___
4	___
5	___

B.

6	4	1
3	7	9
8	2	5

PERIOD	TIME
1	___
2	___
3	___
4	___
5	___

C.

8	10	4	15
14	3	11	5
12	16	7	2
1	6	13	9

PERIOD	TIME
1	___
2	___
3	___
4	___
5	___

Picture Of Ideas

OBJECTIVE: To introduce topics in an enjoyable way.

PROCEDURE:
1. Prior to the session, decide on a picture that participants might draw that will generate thought about the topic. For example, in a management development program, you might ask participants to draw pictures of their organizations which show all the things they must manage.

2. Early in the training program have the participants draw the picture, using materials you provide. Encourage shy or reticent artists by saying that it is the content or idea that counts, not the quality of artwork.

3. Have each person exchange his or her drawing with someone else.

4. Ask each participant to "grade" the drawing he or she just received by assigning an A, B, C, etc. to the drawing. The grade should be based on how completely the drawing captures the intended idea, not on the artistic quality.

5. Ask several of the participants whose drawings were graded A (this is frequently most of the drawings) to show their drawings to the entire group and to describe the ideas behind their drawings. During this series of mini-presentations, add to or emphasize the key ideas about the topic that are triggered by the drawings. Frequently, serious and complex ideas are introduced through the drawings in a setting which includes good-natured ribbing and laughter.

ALTERNATE
PROCEDURE: Provide a broad array of pictorial magazines, and let the participants cut out items of their choice and glue them on paper to create collages that communicate their story. Or, if you wish, steps 3 and 4 may be skipped to save time.

MATERIALS
REQUIRED: Large sheets of paper, plus crayons and felt-tip pens.

APPROXIMATE
TIME
REQUIRED: Thirty-sixty minutes.

SOURCE: Dr. Ed Kur, Arizona State University, Tempe, Arizona

Crossword Puzzles

OBJECTIVE: To provide a distinctive opportunity for reinforcement of newly-acquired technical terms, concepts, and vocabulary.

PROCEDURE:

1. Select the most important new terms that were introduced in the course or module. Develop brief identifying phrases or definitions for each.

2. Construct a simple crossword puzzle that incorporates each of the chosen words, and fill in the appropriate numbers.

3. Present the puzzle and clues to each trainee, with a time limit for its completion. The options here include:

   a. Allowing individual or group work;

   b. Allowing it to be completed on a take-home (overnight) basis;

   c. Allowing use of all reference materials versus a closed-book approach.

MATERIALS
REQUIRED: Prepared list of vocabulary terms and meanings.

APPROXIMATE
TIME
REQUIRED: One minute per term presented, plus scoring time.

SOURCE: F. N. Peare, St. James Hospital, Chicago Heights, Illinois.

Jeopardy

OBJECTIVE:

To provide a competitive environment for the re-inforcement of lessons taught in the previous sessions.

PROCEDURE:

1. Separate trainees into two groups.

2. Develop sets of test questions, organized in categories according to the lessons that have been previously taught.

3. Allow one team to select a category, and ask them a question. If they are successful, award a point (or play money may be used). If they are incorrect, the other team gets a chance to answer, and may thus earn points. If neither team gets it correctly, they must look it up in the course reference material.

4. The first group to accumulate a specified number of points is declared the winner (and some recognition or prize should be awarded).

5. The major benefits provided by this format are:

   a. Repetition of key learning points;

   b. Reinforcement of effective learning;

   c. Feedback to the instructor regarding the points learned well, and those on which there was difficulty on recall.

MATERIALS
REQUIRED:

Previous preparation of test questions; prize.

APPROXIMATE
TIME
REQUIRED:

Twenty-thirty minutes.

SOURCE:

Dolores E. Verdi, AT&T, New Brunswick, N. J.

Managing Your Own Learning

OBJECTIVE: To dramatize the fact that trainees are largely responsible for their own learning process.

PROCEDURE: Inform the trainees that they will be assigned a major responsibility for the management of their own learning in the workshop. Further, they should be aware of, and use, the resources immediately available to them (their peers).

Engage in no climate-building activities. Simply communicate the learning objectives for the session, explain the resources available, clarify the time constraints, and leave the room.

Upon your return, you may wish to facilitate a discussion of what transpired, and the significance of the process for their future learning. In particular, trainees should be encouraged to think ahead to the role they must play in transferring the training to their own work environment at the end of the course.

DISCUSSION
QUESTIONS:
1. Describe the process that took place.
2. Why do you suppose we did this?
3. What did you learn from the experience?

MATERIALS
REQUIRED: None.

APPROXIMATE
TIME
REQUIRED: No additional time.

SOURCE: Bob Humphreys, AT&T, Cincinnati, Ohio.

Learning By Association

OBJECTIVE: To demonstrate that trainee learning takes place more efficiently if the material to be learned is presented in a fashion that allows trainees to see logical patterns that facilitate association of like objects.

PROCEDURE:

1. Inform trainees that they will be asked to memorize the names of twenty common home-related objects in a very brief time period.

2. Divide the class into two groups and provide each group with a different set of instructions.

3. Provide group A with a sheet of paper on which are printed the randomized set of items on the following page. Tell them that they have two minutes from the time they begin in which to learn as many as possible.

4. Provide group B with a sheet of paper on which are printed the same set of items, but organized into implicit groups by room (e.g., living room, kitchen, bedroom, bathroom, and garage). Tell them that they have two minutes from the time they begin in which to learn as many as possible.

5. Provide two minutes to each group to learn the items, and then administer a brief quiz by asking them to write as many of the items as possible on a sheet of paper. Score the results and compute a mean score for each group.

DISCUSSION QUESTIONS:

1. Which group scored the highest? Why?

2. What are the implications for you in your job of this little demonstration of learning by association?

MATERIALS REQUIRED: Preprinted sets of items.

APPROXIMATE TIME REQUIRED: Ten-fifteen minutes.

SOURCE: Jack Hanson, State of Georgia Department of Education, Atlanta, Georgia.

LEARNING BY ASSOCIATION

INSTRUCTIONS: GROUP A:

SOFA, DISH, BED, SINK, CAR, CHAIR, CUP, LAMP,

TOWEL, RAKE, DESK, FORK, DRESSER, SOAP, WHEEL-

BARROW, MIRROR, CLOSET, TUB, BICYCLE, COFFEE

TABLE.

GROUP B:

SOFA, CHAIR, DESK, COFFEE TABLE;

DISH, CUP, FORK, SINK;

BED, LAMP, DRESSER, CLOSET;

TOWEL, SOAP, MIRROR, TUB;

CAR, RAKE, WHEELBARROW, BICYCLE.

Tackling A Can Of Squirms

OBJECTIVE:

To provide opportunities for participants to practice newly learned principles.

PROCEDURE:

Squirms are defined as those problems that make your trainees (e.g., salespeople, supervisors, or customer service personnel) squirm when they are encountered, due to the inherent difficulty involved. Prepare a comprehensive array of these in advance of the session and place them on printed cards in a large can.

After presentation of preliminary materials to guide the trainees (preferably including some modeling), select two "volunteers" and designate the others as observers. Have one person role play the problem person described, while the other attempts to confront and solve the problem. After the attempt has been made, stop the interaction and ask the observers to comment constructively on the interaction. Then proceed to select a second set of actors, and another squirm to encounter.

DISCUSSION
QUESTIONS:

1. What principles did you see demonstrated in the interaction here?

2. What suggestions could you make for improved handling of this situation?

3. What other situations are similar to this?

MATERIALS
REQUIRED:

Previously-created set of common "squirms".

APPROXIMATE
TIME
REQUIRED:

Variable, depending on the complexity of the squirms and the number of incidents to be handled.

SOURCE:

Leonard Zell, Zell Brothers, Portland, Oregon.

III.

BRAINTEASERS

Brainteasers

OBJECTIVE: A "just for fun" series of exercises that can be
used for quick activity or change of pace.

PROCEDURE: Reproduce any of the following pages for each
participant. Suggest that each block represents
a saying or well-known phrase.

MATERIALS
REQUIRED: Handout sheets.

APPROXIMATE
TIME
REQUIRED: Five minutes.

SOURCE: Varied.

DIRECTIONS: Each block represents a saying or well-known phrase.
Please write your answers on the back of the page.

1 PL**OT**	2 WAY ―――― PASS	3 A CHANCE N	4 NOITANIMIRCSID
5 GONE GONE LET BE GONE GONE	6 GETTING IT ALL	7 LU CKY	8 PRE4SS
9 ME ―――――――― IT IT IT IT IT IT IT	10 world	11 chicken	12 WHEATHER
13 GET A WORD IN	14 O MD BA PhD	15 late never	16 ALL /WORLD

89

ANSWERS:

1. The plot thickens
2. Highway overpass
3. An outside chance
4. Reverse discrimination
5. Let bygones be bygones
6. Getting away from it all
7. Lucky break
8. Foreign press
9. It's below me
10. As the world turns
11. Chicken little
12. Bad spell of weather
13. Getting a word in edgewise
14. Three degrees below zero
15. Better late than never
16. Small world after all

DIRECTIONS: Each block represents a saying or well-known phrase.
                   Please write your answers on the back of the page.

1	2	3	4 SHAPE
NIGHT FLY	HE'S/HIMSELF	r o rail d	OR SHIP

5 TROUBLE	6	7	8
T T R R O O U I'M U B B L L E TROUBLE E	Y FIREWORKS	L D BRIDGE	F I D D L E R

9	10	11	12
K PAC✗	DANC T E S C ETNO	LO OSE	MAN BOARD

13	14	15	16
SOUP	WEAR LONG	R/E/A/D/I/N/G	LE VEL

ANSWERS:

1. Fly by night
2. He's beside himself
3. Railroad crossing
4. Shape up or ship out
5. I'm surrounded by trouble
6. Fourth of July fireworks
7. London Bridge
8. Fiddler on the Roof
9. Change of pace
10. Square dance contest
11. Loose at both ends
12. Man overboard
13. Split pea soup
14. Long underwear
15. Reading between the lines
16. Split level

DIRECTIONS: Each block represents a saying or well-known phrase.
                   Please write your answers on the back of the page.

1 SEARCH AND	2 5KATINg	3 OHOLENE	4 RAILROAD
5 $\dfrac{END}{END}$	6 1 at 3:46	7 000 circus	8 HOROOMTEL MOROOMTEL INN

9   BREED
 	
BREED
BREED
BREED
	10
	 E E E E
	    E E
	   E E
	  E E
		11 market the	12
			
			THE END

13 LA ✠	14 T O E A R T H	15 TRIUMPH	16 STEP ——————— STEP STEP STEP STEP

ANSWERS:
1. Search high and low
2. Figure skating
3. Hole in one
4. Elevated railroad
5. End over end
6. One at a time
7. Three ring circus
8. No room at the inn
9. A breed apart
10. The greatest of ease
11. The corner market
12. Beginning of the end
13. Lacrosse
14. Down to earth
15. Arc de Triomphe
16. A step above the rest

DIRECTIONS: Each block represents a saying or well-known phrase.
               Please write your answers on the back of the page.

1 POCHICKENT POCHICKENT POCHICKENT POCHICKENT	**2** ECAP PACE	**3** GUN, JR.	**4** PARKED/PARKED
5 CHECK CHECK CHECK	**6** HEAVENS - PENNIES	**7** COUNTRY COUNTRY	**8** C R ☺ WD
9 DANCER	**10** FISHING c	**11** B A E DUMR	**12** TAKE 1 MEAL TAKE 1 MEAL TAKE 1 MEAL TAKE 1 MEAL
13 V I O L E T s	**14** R ( ) A I)	**15** PEP P PEP P PEP P E PEP PEP PEP PEP PEP PEP P PEP PEP PEP P PEP PEP E PEP PEP E PEP PEP PEP P PEP PEP PEP PEP E P PEP P E	**16** **agb**

ANSWERS:
1. A chicken in every pot
2. Pace back and forth
3. Son of a gun
4. Doubleparked
5. Check and double-check
6. Pennies from heaven
7. Cross country
8. A face in a crowd
9. Topless dancer
10. Deep sea fishing
11. Bermuda Triangle
12. Take one before every meal
13. Shrinking violets
14. Middle of the road
15. Full of pep
16. A mixed bag

DIRECTIONS: Each block represents a saying or well-known phrase.
                Please write your answers on the back of the page.

1 FORGOTTE	2 JIG	3 GRFOOTAVE	4 **THAT**

5
 	
    0
 	
    T V
	6
	
	TIMING TIM ING
		7
		
		YYY MEN
			8 0
			
			SILVER

9 BRETH	10 MOMANON	11 N O T T YOUR U —— B COAT	12 HER ROPE SHE
13 OPERATOR ———— C C C C CC C	14 YOU JUST ME	15 **BALL**	16 HISTORY HISTORY HISTORY

ANSWERS:

1. Almost forgotten
2. The jig is up
3. One foot in the grave
4. Fancy that
5. There is nothing on TV
6. Bad timing
7. Three wise men
8. Hi-O-Silver
9. Short of breath
10. Man in the Moon
11. Button up your overcoat
12. She's at the end of her rope
13. Overseas operator
14. Just between you and me
15. Football
16. History repeats itself

Each block represents a saying or well-known phrase.
Please write your answers on the back of the page.

1 **Hopes**	2 ESROH RIDING	3 S M O K E	4 FALL ALOHA SUMMER HI WINTER HELLO SPRING SHALOM
5 TEEXAMRM	6 **T.V.**	7 LISTING LISTING LISTING LISTING	8 PERSON
9 FORGOTTE	10 T P G S P N E I	11 1. FEET 2. HANDS 3. FACE	12 **SKIING**

13
 	
LEFT ....PRICE
	14
	
	ME/REPEAT
		15
		   Y L I
		R B
		A R
		R A
		 B R
		  I L Y
			16
			
			BONBNET

ANSWERS:

1. Dashed hopes
2. Horseback riding
3. Column of smoke
4. Season's Greetings
5. Midterm exam
6. Black and white T.V.
7. Multiple listing
8. Outgoing person
9. Almost forgotten
10. Stepping out of line
11. Feet first
12. Downhill skiing
13. The price is right
14. Repeat after me
15. Circulating library
16. Bee in a bonnet

How Observant Are You?

OBJECTIVE: To demonstrate to participants that we often overlook many of the details in the objects and events in our daily life unless we force ourselves to become observant.

PROCEDURE: Ask each participant to take a sheet of paper and number from 1-8.   Then ask them these eight questions:

1. What color stripe is directly under the blue field on the U. S. flag? (White)

2. If quotation marks are considered as commas, is the first pair upside down or right side up? (Upside down)

3. Is the full moon high or low in a June sky in the U. S.? (Low)

4. What building is shown on the five dollar bill? (Lincoln Memorial)

5. Which king on the standard playing card is shown in profile? (Diamond)

6. What is the smallest division on the standard (non-metric) ruler? (1/16 inch)

7. How long is the standard cigarette? (2 3/4 inch)

8. Is the coin return on the right or left side of the pay telephone? (Left)

After scoring the eight items, ask for a show of hands to indicate how many got all eight, seven, six, etc. correct. Then discuss how we often overlook small details in our daily environment, and how there is significant benefit from sharpening our observational skills.

MATERIALS
REQUIRED: None, unless you wish to pre-print the test.

APPROXIMATE
TIME
REQUIRED: Ten minutes.

SOURCE: Unknown.

Trivia Quiz

OBJECTIVES:

1. To subtly determine trainees' level of knowledge.

2. To inject a touch of levity into the testing process.

PROCEDURE:

Following the presentation of new material, announce that you will now give a short quiz on the information covered. Distribute the prepared quiz, in which you have interspersed (e.g., odd/even) a set of outrageously trivial questions with a set of legitimate questions. Sample trivia questions include:

1. What is the length of a dollar bill (in centimeters)? (Answer: 15 1/2)

2. How many matches are in a book? (Answer: 20)

3. At what temperature are Fahrenheit and Centigrade equal? (Answer: -40°)

4. What is a group of lions called? (Answer: Pride)

5. How many full moons are there in a year? (Answer: 13)

6. How do they put lead into a pencil? (Answer: they make two halves, insert the lead and glue it together.)

7. What letter does the greatest number of words in the dictionary begin with? (Answer: S)

When all are completed, solicit sample answers to each question from the group. Then obtain a rough count of the error rate via a show of hands. This process will not only take the pressure off those being tested, it will also reduce the likelihood of the trainer being disliked in association with the testing process.

MATERIALS
REQUIRED:

Printed handout or prepared transparency.

APPROXIMATE
TIME
REQUIRED:

Fifteen minutes.

SOURCE:

Bill Allen, Nestle, Canada; Don Mills, Ontario.

IV.

PERCEPTION

Male/Female Perceptions

OBJECTIVE: To increase our awareness regarding possible stereotypical attitudes about male/female behaviors and to illustrate the power of cultural conditioning and stereotyping.

PROCEDURE: Form groups of five-seven. Have each group member list ten behaviors he/she perceived as negative or aggravating, five that are primarily male and five that are primarily female.

When lists are completed, compare with other group members, paying particular attention to specific behaviors, e.g., why you think them negative, why you deem them more peculiar to one sex or the other, and any similarities for and from both sexes.

ALTERNATE
PROCEDURE: Instead of negative behaviors you may ask for five symbols that are primarily male and five female. Each person must explain the meaning of the symbol and why it was chosen. The same discussion questions may be used.

DISCUSSION
QUESTIONS:

1. Are there any similarities in negative male and female behaviors? In male/female perceptions?

2. Which behavior is most aggravating to you? Does sex play a role in the aggravation? (Example: poor drivers)

3. When both sexes are guilty of a negative behavior are you more aggravated by one or the other of the sexes? Why? Why not? Do you notice it more?

4. Could you do this same exercise with positive behaviors?

5. How does this exercise address stereotypes?

MATERIALS
REQUIRED: Pencil and paper.

APPROXIMATE
TIME
REQUIRED: Twenty minutes.

SOURCE: Jacqueline V. Markus, Department of Communication, Arizona State University, Tempe, Arizona.

The Hidden Triangles

OBJECTIVE:

To discourage trainees from jumping to early conclusions before careful analysis of the total picture from many angles.

PROCEDURE:

Display the figure from the following page to the group. Direct them to count the number of triangles portrayed there. After a few minutes, ask for audience reports on how many they found in the diagram. Then proceed to explain that there are a total of 35, as follows:

KEY:

1. There are 10 small single triangles (without any intersecting lines in them, e.g., AFG);

2. There are 5 tall triangles (each with an external side as a base, and containing 5 pieces, e.g., ABD);

3. There are 5 long-base triangles (each with 3 pieces, e.g., ACJ);

4. There are 5 with two exterior sides (each with 3 pieces, e.g., EAB);

5. There are 10 with 2 small triangles inside, e.g., ABF.

DISCUSSION QUESTIONS:

1. Why didn't each of you discover all 35 triangles on your own?

2. How does the lack of a systematic approach cause us problems in our work/personal lives?

MATERIALS REQUIRED:

Transparency and overhead projector or flip chart.

APPROXIMATE TIME REQUIRED:

Five-ten minutes.

SOURCE:

James Ramseyer, Dow Corning, Midland, Michigan.

THE HIDDEN TRIANGLES

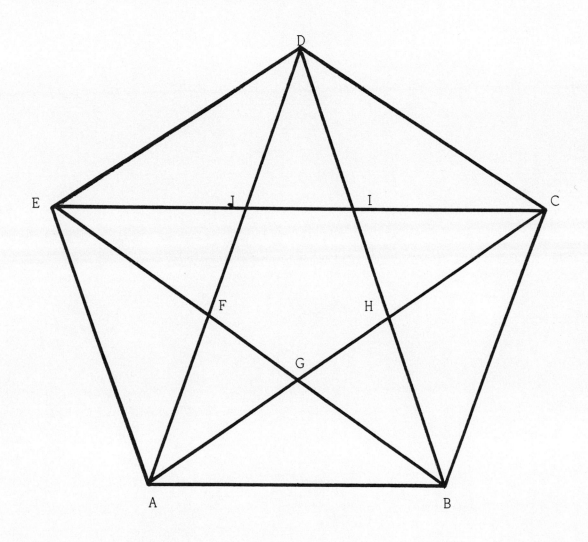

Personality Types

OBJECTIVE: To encourage participants to relax; to introduce the concept that people differ in important ways.

PROCEDURE: Distribute (or display) a copy of the four geometric shapes shown on the following page. Direct each participant to select the one that best represents his/her personality. Ask for a show of hands to determine how many selected 1, 2, 3, and 4. Then proceed (with great seriousness) to suggest that extensive research has shown the following characteristics to be associated with each shape:

1. This person is intellectual, objective, rational, and a good decision-maker.

2. This person is steady, dependable, conservative, and has perseverance.

3. This person is dissatisfied with the status quo, believes in no-nonsense behavior, and tends to be a risk-taker.

4. This person is strongly preoccupied with sex. (This interpretation will invariably evoke a solid round of laughter.)

DISCUSSION
QUESTIONS:

1. In what ways are people really different?

2. Is it possible to categorize people by such a "test"?

3. What are the dangers of stereotyping people?

MATERIALS
REQUIRED: A handout, transparency, or flip chart.

APPROXIMATE
TIME
REQUIRED: Five minutes.

SOURCE: Unknown.

PERSONALITY TYPES

DIRECTIONS: Study the geometric shapes below. Select the one
                that best represents your personality. Place an
                "X" below the chosen one.

1.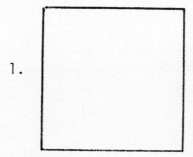

2.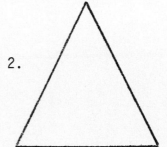

3.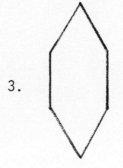

4.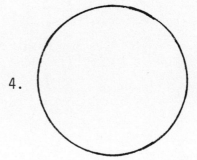

The Perceptual "K"

OBJECTIVE: To impress your participants that "the eye sees, but the mind evaluates."

PROCEDURE:
1. Exhibit the following diagram on a flip chart or chalkboard.

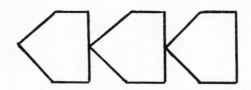

2. Ask your group "What do you see?" Chances are you'll get responses like "arrows", "home plates", "three houses on their side", etc.

3. When you get the response "two K's", immediately highlight the two K's and go on with the exercise by exhibiting the second diagram.

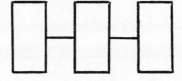

Then ask them "Now what do you see?" Very likely, you'll get the response "two H's". Now ask the group "Would you have seen the H's if someone had not first pointed out the K's?"

DISCUSSION QUESTIONS:
1. Why did you see the H's more easily than the K's? (You were conditioned. The eye sees, but the mind evaluates.)

2. In your work with people, in what ways is your eye seeing one thing and your mind another?

MATERIALS REQUIRED: Flip chart/chalkboard.

APPROXIMATE TIME REQUIRED: Five minutes.

SOURCE: United Air Lines Main Event Management adapted to the Dana Corporation management workshops by Larry F. Lottier, Jr., Toledo, Ohio.

Remodeling A Window

OBJECTIVE: To illustrate to the participants how different
              perceptions lead to breakdowns in communication.

PROCEDURE: Relate to the group that you bought an older home and
              began to remodel one of the rooms. However, you noted
              that one window, which measured two feet horizontally
              and two feet vertically, let in an inadequate amount of
              light. Seeking a resolution to this problem, you took
              your saw and made the opening larger. With pride you
              surveyed your work, noting that a significantly increased
              amount of sunlight now poured through to brighten the room.
              However, when you again measured the dimensions of the
              window you found that it still scaled out to two feet by
              two feet. How do you explain such a phenomenon?

KEY: Ask the group to identify what a "window" is in their
              minds. (Generally, it is a square or rectangular opening
              through which light is allowed to pass.) Then proceed to
              show them the diamond-shaped window on the following page.
              Demonstrate how the window could be enlarged by converting
              it into a square or circle that still measures two feet by
              two feet. The key resides in our perception of what con-
              stitutes a "window"!

DISCUSSION
QUESTIONS: 1. What other common words have multiple meanings,
                  leading to possible confusion in their usage
                  unless clarified?

              2. What can you do to prevent these problems or reduce
                  their likelihood and impact?

MATERIALS
REQUIRED: Transparency of the "key", or use of a flip chart or
              chalkboard.

APPROXIMATE
TIME
REQUIRED: Five minutes.

SOURCE: Dr. Allen R. Solem; and M. R. Miller, Phillips Petroleum
              Company, Bartlesville, Oklahoma.

REMODELING A WINDOW ILLUSTRATED

ORIGINAL:

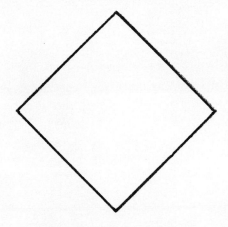

REMODELED:

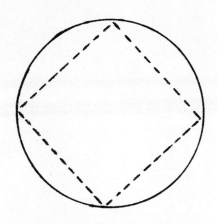

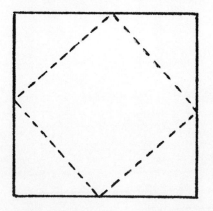

Perception Exercise

OBJECTIVE: To illustrate that people see things differently.

PROCEDURE: Introduce the exercise by stating that often our eyes
may deceive us. These examples of "Optical Art" shown
on the following pages may be used as shown or with
transparencies and overhead projector.

DISCUSSION
QUESTIONS:

1. In Illustration A, is the box inside a room or
    are there two boxes? (Yes! Either is correct.)

2. In Illustration B, are the lines pulled apart
    at the center or are they parallel? (parallel)

3. In Illustration C, what happened to the center
    prong?

4. In Illustration D, which end is out? (either one)

5. In Illustration E, which boy is tallest? (all
    same)

MATERIALS
REQUIRED: Transparencies and overhead projector.

APPROXIMATE
TIME
REQUIRED: Five-ten minutes.

SOURCE: 3-M Company (Used with permission)

ILLUSTRATION A:

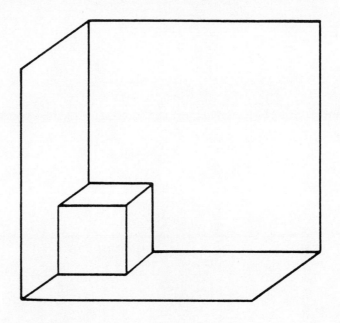

ILLUSTRATION B:

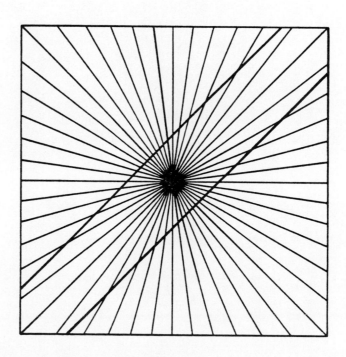

ILLUSTRATION C:

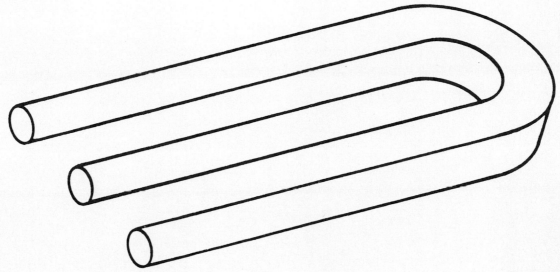

ILLUSTRATION D:

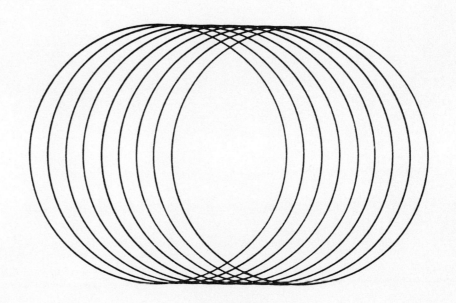

ILLUSTRATION E:

Fact vs. Inference

OBJECTIVE:
To illustrate the difference between statements of fact (descriptions of observations) and statements of inference or opinion.

PROCEDURE:
Hold up an ordinary object (it may be a fountain pen, piece of clothing, textbook, piece of fruit, etc.). Ask participants to make statements of fact about the object. Record statements on the board. After getting about ten or so items, point out that any that go beyond that which can be observed are inferences. Then ask what differences knowing and applying these might make during discussions.

DISCUSSION QUESTIONS:

1. What are the major differences between statements of fact, opinion and/or inference?

   (Statements of fact are: limited to description; made only after observation; are limited in the number that can be made; and, if primary, can be made only by a direct observer.

   Statements of inference: go beyond what was directly observed; can be made at any time without observation; can be made by anyone, observer or not; are unlimited in number about anything; and entail some degree of probability of inferential risk or uncertainty.)

2. Why is it especially important, both in gathering data and evaluating it during discussion, to distinguish between statements of inference or fact? (Recognize the danger for misunderstanding and ineffective communication when statements of inference are acted upon as if they were facts.)

3. Should both statements of fact and inference be treated with the same degree of certainty? (no) Why? Why not?

MATERIALS REQUIRED:
Any handy item, e.g., pen, book, etc.

APPROXIMATE TIME REQUIRED:
Fifteen-thirty minutes.

SOURCE:
Jacqueline V. Markus, Department of Communication, Arizona State University, Tempe, Arizona, adapted from the Instructors Manual, EFFECTIVE GROUP DISCUSSION, 4th Edition, John Brilhart.

Perception

OBJECTIVE:
To illustrate the difficulty in seeing things as others may see them.

PROCEDURE:
Distribute copies of the illustration shown. Let group pass picture around. Do not identify the picture in any way, or even indicate which is the top or bottom side of the illustration.

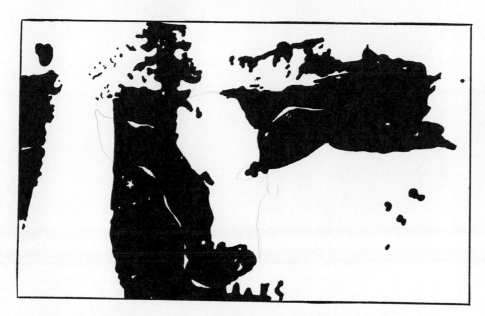

After a few minutes, direct the attention of the group to the right side of the picture and help them ferret out the illustration of the calf head looking straight ahead. Illustrations on next page.

MATERIALS
REQUIRED:
Illustration as shown.

APPROXIMATE
TIME
REQUIRED:
Ten minutes.

SOURCE:
Sidney J. Parnes, State University of New York College at Buffalo, Buffalo, New York.

ILLUSTRATIONS:

V.

COMMUNICATION

Back-To-Back Communication

OBJECTIVE:
To encourage open communications and to illustrate how words, when not coupled with face-to-face contact, are susceptible to incorrect assumptions and interpretations.

PROCEDURE:
Arrange subgroups of five-seven people each. Place two chairs back to back and select or request two people to sit in the chairs. Ask one of these to describe to the other a humorous or silly thing that happened to them. The incident could be recent or some time ago (e.g., When I was learning to drive...). As the one person speaks, the other person is asked to listen intently as he/she will report back to the group. The balance of the participants observe the facial expressions, gestures, nonverbal movements, etc.

DISCUSSION QUESTIONS:

1. As observers, did you tend to see and hear the same message? Why not?

2. As speakers or listeners, how did it feel knowing your words and actions were being closely monitored? In real-life situations, how do you handle this?

3. Communication is often difficult. In cases like this, how can we ensure more effective communications?

MATERIALS REQUIRED:
None.

APPROXIMATE TIME REQUIRED:
Ten minutes.

SOURCE:
Unknown.

Nonverbal Introduction

OBJECTIVE: To be used as a brief get-acquainted exercise.

PROCEDURE: Used best in groups of less than 30 participants, this activity is a light way for mutual introductions. The group is broken into dyads and each person is to "interview" his/her partner and gather whatever information can be gained. The interview, however, is strictly NONVERBAL! No questions, comments or any kind of oral communication is allowed.

Encourage each person to be creative and innovative in soliciting and providing information. Any transaction is "fair game" as long as it's nonverbal. After allowing about eight-ten minutes of the respective groups to "interview" each other, the actual "introductions" begin. After each person is introduced, individuals may add, delete, or correct any information presented.

After all introductions are completed, critique the entire activity.

DISCUSSION
QUESTIONS:

1. How did you feel when trying to express yourself in this fashion?

2. Were some of your nonverbal gestures misinterpreted? Could this have been avoided?

3. Were you fairly accurate in "reading" the nonverbal cues from your partner? Why or why not?

MATERIALS
REQUIRED: None.

APPROXIMATE
TIME
REQUIRED: Twenty-thirty minutes.

SOURCE: Unknown.

For Your Eyes Only

OBJECTIVE: To tune into impressions we make on visual data alone.

PROCEDURE: Have participants break into dyads. Instruct one person to tell the other a story about his/her childhood. The only restriction is that the storyteller may not vocalize the words used to tell the story (e.g., gestures may be used, but words are to be lip-read by the listener). The listener's task is to check out the accuracy of assumptions made about the storyteller based on visual information alone.

DISCUSSION
QUESTIONS:

1. What was the story that was being told?

2. What nonverbal messages made the listener assume a particular story was being told?

3. What emotions were being portrayed while the story-teller was "speaking"?

4. Why did the listener interpret certain facial expressions, body postures, etc., to be the particular emotions he/she chose?

MATERIALS
REQUIRED: None.

APPROXIMATE
TIME
REQUIRED: Fifteen-twenty minutes.

SOURCE: Contributed by Marty Peck, Tempe, Arizona.

The Trainer's Box

OBJECTIVE: To demonstrate the value of a whole-part-whole approach
               to training and job instruction, and the value of step-
               by-step instructions combined with feedback.

PROCEDURE: Distribute a copy of the pre-cut, unassembled box shown
               on the following page. The first time, tell the group
               that you will explain the entire procedure, and then let
               them perform the task. Do so, while limiting the time
               allowed to three minutes and noting the frustration level
               of the persons having difficulty.

               Repeat the exercise (distribute a new cut out). This
               time (a) explain the entire task, (b) tell and show them
               each step and pause to see that each person accomplishes
               it, and (c) review the entire procedure upon its completion.

               Note: In advance, you should develop a standardized script
               that specifies all the moves required to create the trainer's
               box. (For example, "fold piece A toward C, bending it at
               line B; then fold pieces A and B toward D, bending it at
               line C, etc."). This exercise can also be done without
               the lines (the first time) and then showing the value of
               specific reference points on the second time through the
               exercise.

DISCUSSION
QUESTIONS: 1. How was my approach different between the first time
                   and the second time?

               2. What implications does this demonstration have for
                   your training/coaching/job instructional activities?

MATERIALS
REQUIRED: Two sets of pre-cut handouts; possibly a larger model
               of the box for visual display.

APPROXIMATE
TIME
REQUIRED: Fifteen minutes.

SOURCE: Jonda Rourke, Buffy's Department Store, Long Beach,
               California.

TRAINER'S BOX: CUT-OUT

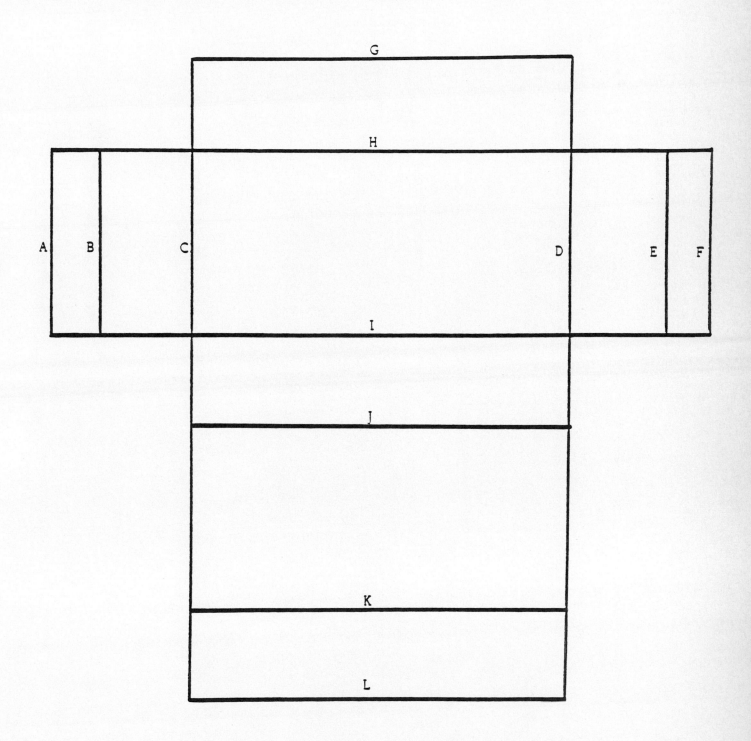

Tearing A Sheet Of Paper

OBJECTIVE: To demonstrate that there is a significant danger to even simple instructions being misinterpreted by the recipient, especially if:

1. Ambiguous words are used; or

2. The recipient does not (or cannot) ask for clarification.

PROCEDURE:

1. Ask the group (e.g., supervisors) if they have ever been misinterpreted by an employee, even if they gave simple instructions. Inquire further how they felt at the time and if they would like to avoid such problems in the future.

2. Select four participants and have them stand in the front of the room, facing the remaining group. Give each of the four a sheet of paper and these two rules: each one must close his/her eyes during the exercise and not ask any questions.

3. Tell them to fold their paper in half and then to tear off the bottom right corner of the paper.

4. Tell them to fold the paper in half again and then to tear off the upper right hand corner.

5. Tell them to fold the paper in half again and then to tear off the lower left hand corner.

6. Instruct them to open their eyes and display the unfolded paper to each other and the audience. (There is a great probability that they will not all be the same.)

DISCUSSION
QUESTIONS:

1. What words in the directions could be interpreted in different ways?

2. How could the directions have been better stated, so as to reduce the ambiguity involved?

3. How can we encourage employees to raise questions for clarification when they don't understand?

MATERIALS
REQUIRED: Several sheets of paper (square sheets are even more interesting, as ingenious participants could choose to fold it from corner to corner, thus creating a triangle).

APPROXIMATE
TIME
REQUIRED: Five minutes.

SOURCE: Russell Dore, Fruehauf Corporation, Detroit, Michigan.

Elegance In Simplicity

OBJECTIVE:

To impress upon trainees that the most effective business communications are written simply so that they can and will be understood. In a nutshell, we should write to express, not to impress.

PROCEDURE:

1. Present a brief lecturette on the value of simplicity in written communications and some of the common rules for attaining such an ideal.

2. Present the following statement to the group and ask them to decipher it quickly:

   "Singular specimen of the scientific class of avis contained within the boundaries of the upper prehensile, is equivalently valuable as a doubled inventory of that item located in a low-spreading thicket."

3. After several minutes of frustrating effort on their part, ask for volunteers to provide the correct interpretation for the class. The answer should be the Ben Franklin adage:

   "A bird in the hand is worth two in the bush."

4. Present a couple of additional examples, having them work in both directions (from complex to simple, as well as simple to complex). You may anticipate that they will let their imaginations take control very quickly.

DISCUSSION
QUESTIONS:

1. Whose needs are served most when we employ complex words and phrases in our communications?

2. What are some potentially dysfunctional consequences of trying to impress others with our sophisticated vocabularies?

MATERIALS
REQUIRED:

Up to a half dozen classic adages, prepared for visible display in both simple and complex form.

APPROXIMATE
TIME
REQUIRED:

Variable, depending on the number of examples used.

SOURCE:

Helen Martin, CUNA Mutual Insurance Group, Madison, Wisconsin.

VI.

PRESENTATION

TOOLS

Sequential Role Play

OBJECTIVE: To get all the participants involved in the role play. Typically, only the players participate; in this variation, everyone could take part.

PROCEDURE: Using a U-shaped or circular seating configuration, brief the group on the problem to be role played. Rather than use only two or three participants, explain that the entire group (20-25 maximum, subgroups of 8-12 are also suggested) will get involved. As the role play starts, each person in round-robin order responds to the comment or statement made by the previous participant. Explain that it is permissable to "pass" if the respective player cannot think of an appropriate response. Continue in sequential order until the role play is completed or if it appears to have served its purpose. A group critique follows.

DISCUSSION
QUESTIONS:

1. Is the technique better--or worse--than the typical role play?

2. What advantages does it offer over regular role play cases? (e.g., more involvement, better attention, etc.)

3. What dangers or disadvantages did it illustrate? (forced attention, possible embarrassment on not being able to respond quickly, etc.)

MATERIALS
REQUIRED: None.

APPROXIMATE
TIME
REQUIRED: Twenty-thirty minutes.

SOURCE: Unknown.

Role Play Follow-Up

OBJECTIVE:

To provide the participants in role play situations with additional information by offering critique on their nonverbal communication.

PROCEDURE:

Before the instructions are given for the participants, select two-three observers and ask them privately to pay special attention to the nonverbal aspects of the players. Invite these observers to jot down several items regarding gestures, facial expressions, etc., that they detect during the actual role play. Encourage the observers to begin their report with some positive and affirmative comments. (If appropriate, ask the role players to comment on their own and the other's body language before the observers are called upon.)

DISCUSSION
QUESTIONS:

1. Did others of you (besides the designated observers) observe the same nonverbal gestures, expressions, etc.? Did you interpret them the same way?

2. Did you notice times when the nonverbals seemed to contradict the verbal parts?

3. Which seemed more effective, the verbal or nonverbal? Why?

MATERIALS
REQUIRED:

None.

APPROXIMATE
TIME
REQUIRED:

Ten-fifteen minutes.

SOURCE:

Unknown.

Unusual Introduction

OBJECTIVE: To offer a different way for an introduction of a trainer or speaker.

PROCEDURE: Before the program or session begins, select four-five participants and provide each with an item or two of background information on the trainer or speaker. The introducer then begins the program by suggesting that the speaker or trainer is probably so well-known that everyone in the audience knows something about his/her background and credentials. The introducer asks, "Tell me, what do you folks know about (speaker's name)?" Then each of the four-five pre-selected people "casually", and without fanfare, states the item or two he or she was given earlier. (This should be done without notes.)

MATERIALS
REQUIRED: Four-five index cards on which is written something about the speaker's background.

APPROXIMATE
TIME
REQUIRED: Three-four minutes.

SOURCE: Unknown.

$86,400 To Spend

OBJECTIVE: To emphasize the importance of time and how to control it.

PROCEDURE: On a board/flip chart, as participants enter the room:

> CONGRATULATIONS TO HARRY
>
> (a name of any participant).

1. Let group talk about what this sign means, in light of the fact that the participant (i.e., Harry) doesn't understand the sign either.

2. After a few minutes, use this script:

   "I really don't know how Harry has remained so calm--because something real exciting happened to him today. His rich uncle has promised to give him $86,400 (write number on board). Now there are some stipulations, because if he does not spend this money wisely, his uncle will write him out of this will. Further stipulations:

   a. Must be spent in next 24 hours;
   b. Stores will be closed a big portion of this time;
   c. He has to work tomorrow because his mean ol' boss won't let him have the day off.

   Harry has agreed to let all of us help spend this money. You can buy anything you want--keep it in even dollars--that you think Harry should have. And Harry--you can buy, too, if you'd like."

Ask participants to call out purchases and prices. Be specific (if it's a car, the make of it; if a house, residential? condo? cabin? where?--and on down the list).

When the $86,400 is spent, ask Harry if he agrees with the purchases (most of the time, changes will be made; be prepared to swing into an explanation of time management if he makes no changes).

Now you're probably all wondering what this has to do with time management. Each of you gets 86,400 seconds-- no more, no less--every day--and how you spend that time, or allow others to spend it for you, is what time management is all about.

MATERIALS
REQUIRED: Board/flip chart and "real" play money can be used as
                    a prop, if preferred.

APPROXIMATE
TIME
REQUIRED: Fifteen minutes.

SOURCE: Willie Cable, Arizona Health Plan, Phoenix, Arizona.

Time To Relax

OBJECTIVE: To be used as a relaxer or stress-reduction exercise. To allow participants to become more aware of themselves and to share feelings and emotions in a non-threatening manner.

PROCEDURE: Ask participants to get themselves into a comfortable position. Tell them to sit back, relax and follow these suggestions that you will read to them:

1. Close your eyes.

2. Tune in to yourself.

3. Become aware of your body.

4. Become aware of your breathing.

5. Feel the air come into your lungs--trace the oxygen through your body until you exhale it.

6. Take three deep slow breaths and feel your body relax more with each breath.

7. Feel your hair--try to sense the actual spot where the hair enters your scalp.

8. Become aware of your hands--are they dry, cold, tense?

9. Tense up your hands--relax them.

10. Three more deep slow breaths and feel your body relax with each breath.

11. Become aware of your little toe. What is it feeling right now? Tighten your toe--relax it.

12. Become aware of your entire body--feel the clothes drapped around your body--feel the air around you.

13. Tense up your entire body--hold it--make it tighter--hold it--relax--take three deep breaths.

14. Tense up your entire body again--hold it--tighter--hold it--tighter--hold it--relax--take three deep breaths.

15. Tense up your entire body again--hold it--tighter--hold it--tighter--hold it--your tightest--relax and take three deep breaths--relaxing more with each breath.

MATERIALS
REQUIRED: None.

APPROXIMATE
TIME
REQUIRED: Ten-fifteen minutes.

SOURCE: Dr. Robert Lindberg, University of Texas at San Antonio,
                         San Antonio, Texas.

Trainer/Trainee Show And Tell

OBJECTIVES:

1. To visually communicate to trainees the four stages of instruction that they will be experiencing.

2. To remind trainers of the different roles that they and their trainees will be playing on an interactive basis.

PROCEDURE:

Explain that you have two objectives for the trainees-- for them to understand HOW to perform an activity, and to be able to DO it. Consequently, you will play two roles--as a classical instructor (to impart knowledge) and as a model (to demonstrate correct behavior and provide feedback). Reproduce for them (via handout or transparency) the model on the following page. Explain the four-step procedure that they will then experience as follows:

1. Trainer explains, trainee listens;

2. Trainer demonstrates, trainee watches;

3. Trainee explains, trainer listens;

4. Trainee performs, trainer watches.

As you progress through each phase, refer them back to the model to remind them of the stage they are in, and your expectations of them.

DISCUSSION
QUESTIONS:

1. Why do you think all four phases are necessary?

2. What is the relationship between knowing and doing?

3. Which phase caused you the most difficulty?

MATERIALS
REQUIRED:

Reproduction of the "Show and Tell" model.

APPROXIMATE
TIME
REQUIRED:

Ten minutes.

SOURCE:

Unknown.

SHOW AND TELL IN TRAINING

ACTOR

TRAINER | 1 | 2 |
TRAINEE | 3 | 4 |

EXPLAIN   PERFORM

ROLE

Candy Is Dandy....

OBJECTIVES:

1. To motivate trainees to participate actively in group discussion.

2. To demonstrate the utility of using valued rewards to motivate people.

PROCEDURE:

Explain the value of thoughtful contributions of ideas as well as questions from the participants in creating a productive learning climate. Express your specific invitation for the trainees to participate in the forthcoming discussion. Explain that they may find themselves reinforced with extrinsic rewards for their contributions, in addition to the intrinsic satisfaction that they will gain from the knowledge that they contributed to another's learning experience.

State a specific topic for discussion purposes and indicate how you have structured it. Present a question or issue to which they may respond. As participants begin to make contributions to the discussion, reward them initially with small candies, and later with larger candy bars. Then visibly place a bottle of liquor on the table or podium and continue the discussion process. Inform them that the next meaningful contribution or answer to a question will be rewarded with the bottle. (You'll be amazed by the rush to respond!) Conclude with the old cliche that says, "Candy is dandy, but liquor is quicker!"

DISCUSSION
QUESTIONS:

1. Why do people respond better when they are rewarded?

2. What are the rewards to which people respond best?

3. Is there any danger of diminishing an intrinsically satisfying behavior by the application of an extrinsic reward? What examples can you think of that demonstrate this?

MATERIALS
REQUIRED:

A supply of individual candy bars (small and large) and a bottle of liquor.

APPROXIMATE
TIME
REQUIRED:

Fifteen minutes, in addition to the basic discussion of the underlying topic.

SOURCE:

Lester Anderson, West Vaco, U. S. Envelope Division, Springfield, Massachusetts.

Stand Up And Pat Down

OBJECTIVE: To create spontaneous breaks in long presentations.

PROCEDURE:

1. Early in the session select one or two "Break Managers" from participants who volunteer for the job. Tell participants that Break Managers will determine when the group will take brief breaks.

2. Whenever the Break Managers believe the participants are getting a bit tired, or that you are getting a bit boring, they are to stand up. This signals others to also stand up (if they'd like) and take a 30-second stretch break. Whenever the Break Managers and others stand up, you momentarily stop your presentation. This generally creates a lot of humor and goodwill with the group and sometimes gives them a chance to tell you (in a good-natured way) they think you're on a tangent.

3. In a long presentation, during the second or third stand-up-break, encourage people to "pat down", that is to massage the backs of their own necks, legs, arms, etc. and to stretch or loosen up physically. This helps people feel more awake and energized.

4. In a very long presentation, during the third or fourth stand-up-break, encourage people to "pat down" or massage one another's shoulders and back. This is usually both fun and refreshing for most participants although those who are more inhibited may choose to take the break without participating in the massage.

MATERIALS
REQUIRED: None

APPROXIMATE
TIME
REQUIRED: Each break takes about one minute.

SOURCE: Adapted by Dr. Ed Kur from games played by Joel Weldon and Jeanie Cochran.

What Kind Of Employee Are You?

OBJECTIVE: To encourage new employees to make advance decisions about the type of person that they intend to become inside the organization.

PROCEDURE: Fill three glasses about three-quarters full of water and place them on the table in view of all participants. Place two aspirin in the first one. Suggest that the lack of any overt response is analogous to a "do-nothing" employee.

Place two Bromo Seltzer in the second glass. Note that this type of employee has a great burst of initial enthusiasm but quickly loses it.

Place two Alka Seltzer in the third glass. Note that this type of employee produces a relatively strong but stable output (and hence is the most desirable).

ALTERNATIVE
PROCEDURE: Explain that there are three types of employees in the work force today. The first type MAKES things happen; the second type WATCHES what happens; and the third type WONDERS what happened! This story is especially effective if illustrated with Retrophane transparency film, in which the first key word (MAKES) can be written on the overhead with permanent ink, while the second and third key words (WATCHES and WONDERS) should be written with their disappearing ink pen. The point can then be vividly demonstrated that only those who MAKE things happen will survive over the long term.

MATERIALS
REQUIRED: Three glasses and the associated tablets, plus a towel for clean-up.

APPROXIMATE
TIME
REQUIRED: Five minutes.

SOURCE: Glen T. Presley, Blue Cross/Blue Shield, Chicago, Illinois

"Faster Than A Speeding Bullet"

OBJECTIVE:

To illustrate the speed of today's technology by demonstrating the fast pace at which things happen.

PROCEDURE:

In most every training session, a discussion on change or the increasing impact of technology can be introduced. This is a simple demonstration that dramatically illustrates how fast things happen in today's world.

Ask for the group's attention as you hold a glass of water above a table. State, "To show you how things have changed and how very quickly things can happen..." Pause and then gently pour some water from the glass on to the table or floor. (Have a towel to catch the water.) Then continue, "In the split second it took the water to reach the table (floor), a large computer could have:

* debited 2,000 checks to 300 bank accounts
* analyzed 100 patients' electrocardiograms
* scored 150,000 answers on 3,000 examinations
* processed a payroll for 1,000 employees.

MATERIALS
REQUIRED:

Glass of water and towel.

APPROXIMATE
TIME
REQUIRED:

One minute.

SOURCE:

Adapted from Eastern Air Lines Review, "Love At First Byte", October 1982.

VII.

CONFERENCE

LEADERSHIP

The Animal Analogy

OBJECTIVE:
To allow trainers, conference leaders, facilitators, etc., to be appraised of their meeting management style in a non threatening way.

PROCEDURE:
At the conclusion of a conference or training meeting, inform the group you would like some feedback on the way you conducted the meeting. Rather than verbal or a written evaluation (or in addition to these forms), ask each participant to sketch out a picture of any animal that might describe the way you led the session. It is important this be kept light, e.g., if you are a task-master, tell the group the previous program attendees gave you three bulls and four elephants!

DISCUSSION QUESTIONS:

1. What are some other ways we could secure this type of feedback?

2. If we're attending a meeting conducted by a bullish taskmaster, what are some ways to tactfully suggest that person change his/her tactics?

3. What would be considered an ideal animal in this exercise? Why?

MATERIALS REQUIRED:
Blank sheets of paper.

APPROXIMATE TIME REQUIRED:
Five minutes.

SOURCE:
Col. Ralph Milstead, Arizona Department of Public Safety.

Even Instructors Err Sometimes

OBJECTIVE: To stimulate participants to focus carefully on what the instructor is doing and saying and to motivate them to reflect on ways that they could improve on what is being taught.

PROCEDURE: The following discussion assumes that you are teaching a session on "effective presentations", but could be equally adaptable to many other topics wherever demonstration is appropriate. It is especially useful in those (frequent!) contexts where some participants feel that they already know most of the answers (and probably do have some expertise).

Begin the session by exhibiting several of the most common mistakes that presenters might make. For example, you might:

1. Be late.

2. Be unorganized.

3. Maintain poor eye contact.

4. Speak in a monotone.

5. Forget to plug in the projector.

6. Not bring enough handouts.

7. Have poor visual aids.

8. Etc.

After about ten minutes of this, stop and have the group identify all the things that you did wrong. These can be listed on a flip chart, followed by discussion of the correct ways to do it. The visual impact of seeing the errors in action is powerful, and it is a useful way to stimulate discussion within the group.

MATERIALS
REQUIRED: None, except for any props (bad visuals, etc.).

APPROXIMATE
TIME
REQUIRED: Twenty minutes.

SOURCE: Ron Babitz, Meijer, Inc., Grand Rapids, Michigan.

Know Your Dictionary!

OBJECTIVE:
To demonstrate that there is often substantial benefit from collaborating in small groups to obtain the answers to certain types of questions.

PROCEDURE:

1. Explain that dictionaries, with their hundreds of thousands of entries, contain sharply different numbers of words beginning with each letter in the alphabet. The task today is to identify which of ten letters is more or less frequently used to begin those words.

2. Working individually, have them rank order from 1-10 the following letters, with 1 designated as the most frequently-used letter to begin words, 2 as the next most, etc.: O, X, M, S, Z, P, J, T, Q, W.

3. Now break them into small groups of three-five persons. Working collaboratively, have them rank-order the same ten letters through the use of the collective wisdom in their group.

4. Now have them score both themselves as individuals, and their groups, by computing the absolute arithmetic difference between their ranking and the "key" for each letter and totalling that set of ten numbers. The correct rank is:

   1=S, 2=P, 3=T, 4=M, 5=W, 6=O, 7=J, 8=Q, 9=Z, 10=X.

DISCUSSION
QUESTIONS:

1. How many persons had a group score better than their individual score?

2. What specific behaviors or actions within the group helped it to perform well?

3. On what type of tasks do groups perform better than individuals?

MATERIALS
REQUIRED:
None, although worksheets for the individual and group rankings could be prepared in advance.

APPROXIMATE
TIME
REQUIRED:
Thirty-forty minutes, plus discussion time.

SOURCE:
Webster's International Dictionary.

Stay On The Ball

OBJECTIVES:

1. To stimulate participants to be attentive and focus on active listening during a discussion.

2. To demonstrate that active involvement in the session by each participant is desired by the trainer and can also be enjoyable.

PROCEDURE:

1. Take out a soft, catchable ball (e.g., a "Nerf" ball). Select a participant and throw it back and forth to one person for a minute or two.

2. After the pattern has been firmly established, invite the other participants to participate. Make sure that the ball passes back and forth among the trainees and only occasionally to yourself. Observe carefully to make sure that no one is neglected and direct the ball to them if it happens. Continue this for a few minutes until a clear pattern of cross-group interaction is established.

3. Engage the group in brief discussion, revolving around the following questions.

DISCUSSION
QUESTIONS:

1. How did you feel when only one person and I were playing catch?

2. Did you observe more spontaneity, smiles, and overall involvement when the entire group was participating? Why?

3. Is there not an important analogy here--that we can learn from each other (not just the trainer), but only if we all agree to become actively involved in both the listening and contributing processes?

MATERIALS
REQUIRED: A soft ball.

APPROXIMATE
TIME
REQUIRED: Five-ten minutes.

SOURCE: M. Kane, Imperial Life Assurance Co., Toronto, Ontario, Canada.

Mixing It Up

OBJECTIVE: To create discussion groups of different composition, with a minimum of confusion, delay, or hard feelings.

PROCEDURE:
1. A classic procedure is to simply announce to the group that you would like them to break into discussion groups of five persons each (for example), and give them a discussion topic or task assignment and the time to complete it.

2. Another approach, especially useful where precision is important in getting the same number of people into each group, is to have the audience "count off". To determine the repetitive number to use for this purpose:

   a. Count the number of people in total (=N).

   b. Determine the number of people that you want to be in each group (=X).

   c. Divide N by X and have the group count off from one up to that number and repeat across the group until everyone has a number.

   d. Instruct each person to locate themselves at a table with all other persons of that number.

3. Another method is to pre-assign a number or letter to each person by writing it on their name tag or tent card. Then, when you wish to break them into new groups, simply request all A's to join together, all B's, all C's, etc.

4. A fourth procedure is to prepare in advance a set of numbered Ping-Pong balls (with the desired allotment of 1's, 2's, 3's, etc.). Then simply announce your desire that they form into groups. Begin to throw out the balls to the participants, until everyone has caught (or retrieved) one. Then direct them to find others with the same number and form into discussion groups.

MATERIALS REQUIRED: Name tags, tent cards, or Ping-Pong balls.

APPROXIMATE TIME REQUIRED: As little as one minute.

SOURCE: Pifter Jagers, Management Center "DeBaak", Noordwyk, Holland.

Feedback Cards

OBJECTIVE: To provide an expeditious method for obtaining comprehensive feedback from a group of trainees.

PROCEDURE: Obtain poster boards with one color on one side and a second color on the other (preferably red and green). Cut them into small squares (approximately four inches per side). Distribute one to each participant.

Inform the group that the cards will be used to provide the trainer with feedback in response to his/her questions. Questions with true/false or yes/no responses work best, with green indicating true or yes, and red reflecting false or no. The entire group should then hold up their cards in response to instructor questions. Not only does this give the instructor immediate feedback on the retention and understanding in the group, but the participants can also be encouraged to look around and determine the degree of agreement with their response.

NOTE: This is also an effective procedure for controlling tangential discussions by participants (or even the instructor!), wherein the group members may indicate their willingness to pursue or truncate the discussion by display of the green (continue) or red (terminate) cards.

MATERIALS
REQUIRED: Cards for each participant.

APPROXIMATE
TIME
REQUIRED: Virtually none.

SOURCE: Dr. Richard Beatty, University of Colorado, and John Price, Prudential House, York, England.

VIII.

LISTENING

Communication Quickies

OBJECTIVE:
To stimulate participants to listen carefully and follow directions.

PROCEDURE:
1. Ask participants to place a clean sheet of paper in front of them.

2. For the first task, ask them to spell out two words from these letters, using all of them: OODRWWTS.

3. For the second task, ask them to identify the letter of the alphabet that logically follows this sequence of seven letters: OTTFFSS.

KEY:
1. The letters (and directions) spell "two words".

2. The next letter is "E", the first letter of "eight", which follows one, two, three, etc.

DISCUSSION QUESTIONS:
1. What did this teach you about the need to listen carefully?

2. What did this teach you about the need to look for meaningful patterns in the clues given us by others?

MATERIALS REQUIRED:
Sheets of paper.

APPROXIMATE TIME REQUIRED:
Five minutes.

SOURCE:
Bob Ley, IBM Corp., Franklin Lakes, New Jersey.

Listening With Interest

OBJECTIVE: To show that listening can be improved when one's interest is induced. To further illustrate that most of us listen at a relatively low level of efficiency on matters of little or no interest.

PROCEDURE: Take any article (two-three paragraphs) from a magazine or newspaper. The article should be of a non-business nature and preferably one in which most attendees would have little interest.

With little introduction, read the article to the group. Upon finishing, ask the group to write down three-four things they heard.

Then read an article (three-four paragraphs) from a trade journal or magazine in which most participants can identify with, i.e., their organization, city, or other such area of interest. After reading this to them, again ask them to write down as much as they can remember about the story. Compare the results.

DISCUSSION
QUESTIONS:

1. Why did most of us "flunk" the first quiz? (no interest, "why bother," no purpose etc.)

2. Research shows that immediately upon hearing something, most of us forget 50% just that fast. Why then, in the second example, did many of us score so well?

3. What additional barriers to listening does this illustrate?

MATERIALS
REQUIRED: Magazine articles.

APPROXIMATE
TIME
REQUIRED: Five-ten minutes.

SOURCE: Unknown.

Empathetic Listening

OBJECTIVE:

To develop skills of empathy in communication by active and effective listening.

PROCEDURE:

Select a topic of a controversial nature from a magazine or local newspaper. Subjects could be on politics, labor, management or any other topic in good taste.

Subdivide participants into groups of three. Each triad selects a Speaker, Listener, and Referee. The selected topic is discussed by the Speaker who, without interruption, explains his/her feelings on that topic. After the Speaker has finished, the Listener summarizes (without notes) what was said on the subject. Following this segment, Speaker and Referee can correct or amplify any item stated by the Listener. The Referee is the only person allowed to use notes.

After an eight-ten minute discussion, select a new topic and reverse roles, using the same procedure. After eight-ten minutes, another new topic and role reversals are used, thus allowing each person to act in each of the three roles.

DISCUSSION
QUESTIONS:

1. In your role as Speaker, did you sense any difficulties or experience any awkward moments?

2. How about as Listener or Referee?

3. Did you identify or observe any barriers that obstructed effective listening?

4. In your role as Listener, why was it difficult to summarize and paraphrase the Speaker's comments?

MATERIALS
REQUIRED:

Newspaper or magazine articles as needed.

APPROXIMATE
TIME
REQUIRED:

Twenty-thirty minutes.

SOURCE:

Unknown.

First Person Pronouns

OBJECTIVE: To improve listening skills and become more aware of conversational habits.

PROCEDURE: Divide into pairs. Hold a conversation without using any personal pronouns. When one individual uses "me" or "I" or "we", he/she is eliminated. Last two persons left go to the front of the group to have the last conversation. Award some small token or have group simply clap for "winner". You'd be surprised how difficult it is not to talk about yourself.

DISCUSSION
QUESTIONS:

1. The word "you" is said to be the most important word in our language. Why don't we use it more often?

2. Why do we find it so awkward or difficult to lessen the "I's, me's, mine, etc." in daily conversations?

3. Are there ways we can persuade our trainees (or bosses) to also rely more on the "you" part of conversation?

MATERIALS
REQUIRED: None.

APPROXIMATE
TIME
REQUIRED: Moves quickly; no time limit.

SOURCE: Margaret C. Baldwin, New Orleans, Louisiana.

Willing Self To Listen: Can You?

OBJECTIVE: To explain and exemplify the difficulty of listening to messages.

PROCEDURE: A conversation (telephone, etc.) is taped with different bits of information (either one-way or two-way). After participants listen to the tape, ask six-eight questions on items included in the message. (Experience indicates most people can correctly answer only about half of the questions.) Then play another recording and ask participants to listen intently. Following the recording, again ask six-eight questions. Ask group response on correct answers.

DISCUSSION
QUESTIONS:

1. What barriers to effective listening did this exercise illustrate? (lack of interest or attention, emotions, distractions, etc.)

2. Why was your "listening quotient" better on the second exercise? (attention, test, interest, etc.)

3. How can we motivate others (and ourselves) to listen more attentively?

MATERIALS
REQUIRED: Tape recorded message (20-30 seconds) with names, dates, times, addresses, inferential information, test questions.

APPROXIMATE
TIME
REQUIRED: Ten minutes.

SOURCE: Unknown.

IX.

CREATIVE

PROBLEM

SOLVING

Fun With Names

OBJECTIVE: To be used as a warm-up exercise or to introduce a more intense problem solving activity.

PROCEDURE: On this are listed several people whose names also indicate their profession. By rearranging the letters in their first and last names, you'll discover their line of work. For example, Art Rein is a trainer. Easy, right?

NAME	PROFESSION
1. Art Rein	_____
2. Tim Niser	_____
3. Rae Mang	_____
4. Roy Tenat	_____
5. Brock Kortes	_____
6. Alice V. Staips	_____
7. Janis Roult	_____
8. Chet Incani	_____
9. Ann Stocut	_____
10. Ron Sturcti	_____

MATERIALS
REQUIRED: Handout with the above listed.

APPROXIMATE
TIME
REQUIRED: Five-ten minutes.

SOURCE: Unknown.

ANSWERS:
    1. Trainer

    2. Minister

    3. Manager

    4. Attorney

    5. Stockbroker

    6. A. V. Specialist

    7. Journalist

    8. Technician

    9. Consultant

  10. Instructor

Dot In A Circle

OBJECTIVE:
To encourage participants to solve a task (an apparently impossible one) through the use of creativity.

PROCEDURE:
Participants are provided with a visual drawing of a circle with a dot in the middle (see following page). They are then directed to produce such a figure "without lifting their pencil from the paper".

KEY:
Fold a corner of the paper up toward the middle. Place the pencil lead against the edge of the fold and create a dot adjacent to the fold (and in the middle of the original sheet). Then without lifting the pencil to break contact with the paper, drag the point across the folded corner a few inches and then begin to sweep around the dot to create a circle. As the pencil moves off the folded corner and onto the regular paper surface, unfold it to make room for a complete circle to be drawn. Note that the pencil has remained in continuous contact with the paper.

DISCUSSION QUESTIONS:

1. What prevented you from seeing the solution initially (e.g., a self-definition that "the problem is impossible")?

2. What rule of creativity is involved in the solution (e.g., redefinition of the problem)?

3. How could you use this creative principle at work?

MATERIALS REQUIRED:
Flip chart.

APPROXIMATE TIME REQUIRED:
Five-ten minutes.

SOURCE:
John Turner, Blue Cross.

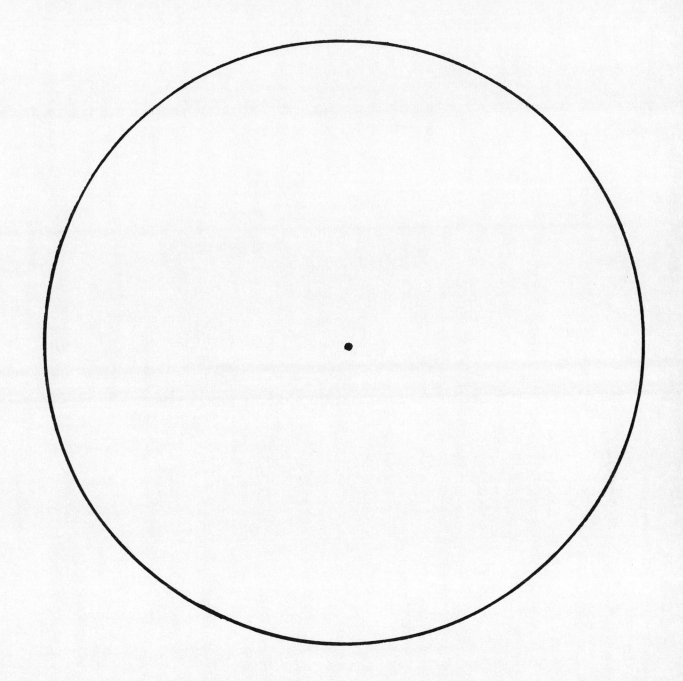

The Easy One

OBJECTIVE: To stimulate participants to approach situations from a problem orientation, not one of forcing a solution.

PROCEDURE: Display the figure on the following page to the audience. Explain that their task is to make the two sides of the equation equal by changing the position of one line. Allow a few minutes for them to experiment. Then solicit solutions from the group. Finally, share the "key" with them.

KEY: At least three solutions exist:

1. Move one line from vertical to horizontal to create a square root sign, such that the square root of 1 = 1.

2. Move one line from the V to a horizontal position such that a divide sign is created, and therefore 1 divided by 1 = 1.

3. Move one line from the V to create a multiplication sign between two vertical lines, such that 1 times 1 = 1.

DISCUSSION QUESTIONS:

1. What factors may have prevented you from seeing one (or all three) of the solutions (e.g., a focus on only one-half of the problem--the right side)?

2. State the principle(s) useful in solving this task (e.g., inventory the known resources of five lines; be cautious about the assumptions you make--that the VII is a 7, for example.)

MATERIALS REQUIRED: Overhead projector, chalkboard, or flip chart.

APPROXIMATE TIME REQUIRED: Five-ten minutes.

SOURCE: Contributed by Larry Lottier, Dana Corp., Toledo, Ohio and George Greey, Arizona State University, Tempe, Arizona.

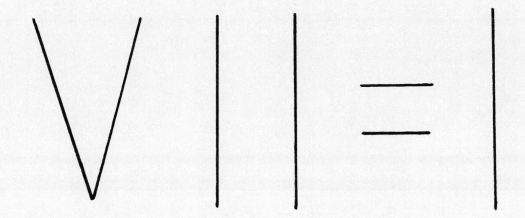

The Nine Dots Puzzle-Revisited

OBJECTIVE: To illustrate the importance of seeking new solutions to old problems.

PROCEDURE: Draw nine dots (as shown here)

. . .

. . .

. . .

on chalkboard, flip chart, or overhead and ask participants to copy. Give these instructions, "Without taking pen or pencil off your paper, connect all nine dots with four straight lines."

Because this exercise has been used for some time, many participants will have seen it. Experience indicates 1/3 to 1/2 of typical audiences will know the answer. Ask the group, "How many have seen this done before?" As they raise their hands, tell them, "O.K. your job is to do it with three straight lines without taking pen or pencil off the page."

The answer is on the next page.

DISCUSSION QUESTIONS:

1. If you had difficulty solving the puzzle, what were some of the constraints? ("boxed in", too difficult, etc.)

2. We often find ourselves constrained or psychologically boxed in on many projects. How can we alleviate this?

3. Can anyone connect all nine dots with just one stroke? (use a paint brush; fold paper so all nine dots are partially superimposed.)

MATERIALS REQUIRED: Chalkboard, flip chart, or overhead.

APPROXIMATE TIME REQUIRED: Five-ten minutes.

SOURCE: Unknown.

As a reminder, the most frequently used solution for touching all nine dots with four straight lines is shown here:

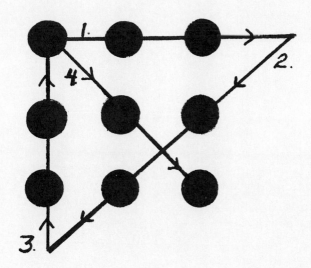

To hit all nine dots with three straight lines, try this solution:

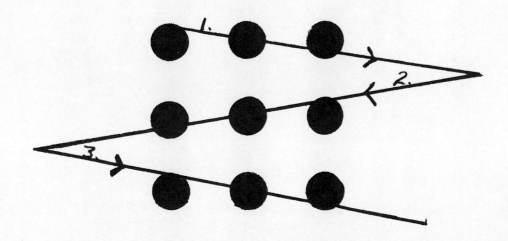

How Many Trees Are In An Apple?

OBJECTIVE: To demonstrate that often it is useful to immerse yourself in a problem before you can see all of its dimensions.

PROCEDURE: Display a picture of an apple tree to the group. Suggest that it is a relatively easy task for anyone to determine the number of apples on a tree (through observation and careful counting). Consequently, the task lends itself to completion on an individual basis.

Some tasks, however, require immersion into them before the answer can be obtained. Distribute an apple to each participant. Ask them to determine how many trees are (potentially) within each apple. The solution, of course, lies in dissecting each apple (they may eat it, if they wish) and counting the number of seeds found.

DISCUSSION
QUESTIONS:

1. What kind of problems have you encountered that are of a similar nature?

2. What techniques have you found useful to aid you in the process of immersion?

MATERIALS
REQUIRED: Picture of an apple tree; one apple per person.

APPROXIMATE
TIME
REQUIRED: Five-ten minutes.

SOURCE: Avery Willis, Baptist Sunday School Board, Nashville, Tennessee.

X.

SELF-CONCEPT

Your Personal Universe

OBJECTIVE: To graphically illustrate each participant's own
                 perception of his or her life.

PROCEDURE: Explain that each of us is the center of his or her own uni-
                 verse. We filter, act on, translate, accept or reject
                 people, information, and ideas based on how we feel or
                 think or respond to their influence on our life/universe.

                 Have each participant draw his or her personal universe,
                 focusing on the time spent "on the job". Picture the
                 "world of work" and all of its facets. Draw the uni-
                 verse using the guidelines listed. Art is not the
                 key--gut level feelings and thoughts are.

                 Encourage the participants to read and do each step
                 in order before moving on to the next step.

INSTRUCTIONS: 1. Using flip chart paper and a colored marker, place
                    a circle in the center of the paper to represent
                    you. Write your name in the circle.

                 2. In the space around you, draw and label other
                    circles to represent people or things that impact
                    you. The size of the circles, and the distance
                    from you, indicate the strength of the impact that
                    person or thing has on you. For example: a very
                    large circle, or a circle placed very close to you
                    indicates a great deal of impact. A small circle,
                    or one on the periphery of your "universe" indi-
                    cates less of an impact.

                 3. Choose another colored marker.

                 4. Next to each of the circles impacting you, place a
                    "+" and/or a "-" to indicate whether the impact is
                    positive or negative (good or bad). Some circles
                    may have only one symbol, while others may have
                    both. The size of the symbol will indicate the
                    strength of the positive or negative influence.
                    Example: a circle has a strong positive influence,
                    and a minor, though irritating, negative influence.
                    You would place a large "+" and a small "-" next
                    to that circle.

                 5. You now need another marker. Pick a color you have
                    not used before.

                 6. Draw arrows between you and the circles impacting
                    you, to indicate whether the influence exerted is

growing or diminishing. For example: if you have recently changed location, and are now geographically separated from your administrator, the influence he/she exerts over your universe is probably diminishing. You would draw the arrow pointing <u>away</u> from you. If a circle has an influence in your universe that is growing, or expanding, the arrow would be drawn pointing toward you. Some arrows may point in both directions.

7. Now that you have drawn your universe, you might want to consider the following:

   a. Have you forgotten someone or something?
   b. Look at the arrows you drew. Do the arrows that move toward you stop at the edge of your circle, inside your circle, or do they pass through your circle? How are the arrows shaped? Are they long, short, straight, or do they have hooks, curves and kinks in them? Why?
   c. Use a pencil or pen, and divide your paper into quarters. Are certain types of impacting circles located more in one quadrant than the others? Are the circles clustered together or spread out?
   d. Are any of the circles bigger than your circle? Do any circles touch or overlap your circle?
   e. Is there some additional factor you would like to show that was not in the instructions? If so, make up a symbol and do it! If you have a marker with a color that you haven't used yet, that's even better, use it.
   f. Now that you have played with and thought about your personal universe; how does it look, and feel, and sound to you, right now?

MATERIALS
REQUIRED: Flip chart paper, three or four different colored magic markers, preprinted instructions, if desired.

APPROXIMATE
TIME
REQUIRED: Thirty-forty minutes.

SOURCE: Catherine L. Moes, Gail D. O'Byrne and Richard A. Robinson, Jr., <u>Mid-Level Management Workshop</u>, State of Washington.

Your Future Universe

INSTRUCTIONS: Now that you have drawn your universe, and spent some
                time thinking about the implications, some issues
                should be apparent to you. Pictorially, you have been
                able to see the opportunities to improve or enhance
                your universe.

                Record the opportunities of your universe. This will
                aid you in getting a more firm grasp of what you want
                and how to attain it. Should you desire to pursue
                these opportunities in the future, this information
                will be most helpful.

                Be sure to label the universe being written about as
                current or future; suggest that the participants pre-
                pare an action plan as follows:

                              OPPORTUNITIES...

                The Issue I Have   The Action(s) Needed
                The Opportunity   To Capitalize On This
                To Enhance Is: Opportunity Is:

                The Assistance I   My Priority For This
                Need To Accomplish   Action Is:
                This Action Is:

MATERIALS
REQUIRED: Flip chart paper, three or four different colored magic
                markers, preprinted instructions, if desired.

APPROXIMATE
TIME
REQUIRED: Thirty-forty minutes.

SOURCE: Catherine L. Moes, Gail D. O'Byrne and Richard A. Robinson,
                Jr., Mid-Level Management Workshop, State of Washington.

A Clear Image

OBJECTIVE: To assist participants in becoming acquainted with one another in an informal setting.

PROCEDURE: Each participant is given a preprinted form as shown on the following page. After being given a few minutes to respond to the questions, ask each participant to introduce themselves. These introductions will reveal "gut-level" values held by the participants.

MATERIALS
REQUIRED: Preprinted forms of "A Clear Image".

APPROXIMATE
TIME
REQUIRED: Thirty-sixty minutes, depending on the size of the group.

SOURCE: Catherine L. Moes and Richard A. Robinson, Jr., Working With Conflicting Values, State of Washington.

A CLEAR IMAGE

In any workshop, one of the most difficult, yet important, steps is to become acquainted with the other participants. To make the job of introducing yourself a little easier, take a few minutes and consider the following statements. We've left space for you to scribble down some thoughts and ideas. It's fair to peek at this later when you are addressing the other people.

1. Who am I?_____

2. What I value most is:_____

3. What motivates me is:_____

4. What I like most about my job is:_____

    _____

5. What I like least about my job is:_____

    _____

6. Money, time, responsibility aside, I would

    rather_____

    _____than anything else.

7. Excluding my parents, if I could choose any two

    people for parents, they would be:_____

    _____

Sugar Gram

OBJECTIVE: To acquaint people with their abilities to give and receive compliments. In minutes the effects are realized--and the socio-emotional climate is enhanced.

PROCEDURE: Each individual is given approximately five minutes to write as many positive compliments, that are honest, to as many people as possible. They can be surface compliments (your tie is nice, your dress looks nice on you, etc.) or they can be more personal, whatever the sender feels comfortable giving. The only other criterion is there must be eye-contact when delivering them. They can be anonymous and folded, but each person must look at the other person when handing them out.

The recipients cannot open any sugar grams until everyone is finished handing them out. Then everyone sits down to "unwrap" their "presents" at the same time.

The facilitator should comment on the general mood present, the nonverbal signals being sent out, the smiles. Prior to reading them, facilitator asks: "How many of you received at least one gram from someone you did not write one to?" "How did it make you feel?" Perhaps that is why so many of us disregard honest compliments--because we respond to just giving out another one, etc...

Everyone opens the grams and the mood is heightened even more. The socio-emotional climate will peak. Some will respond a bit embarrassed, but there will be no denying that the experience was pleasurable.

DISCUSSION QUESTIONS:

1. Why do we limit honest compliments to those we care about, work with, or even observe?

2. How did you feel when reading what people wrote about you?

3. Could you adapt and use this practice as part of your style to become more aware--more receptive?

4. Did the fact they were anonymous have any significance? Why?

5. If you were to match up those with whom you had eye contact and the grams you received, how would you do it? What does that add to that relationship?

6. Are there any additional ones you would like to write? Why not do it on your own when the feeling strikes?

MATERIALS
REQUIRED: Paper, pencils or pens--and some honest giving.

APPROXIMATE
TIME
REQUIRED: Fifteen-twenty minutes.

NOTE: This is great before a break or at the end of a session. Facilitator should prepare a few sugar grams in the event someone may not receive one.

SOURCE: Linda McCay, Arnold/McCay Consultants, Phoenix, Arizona.

Introduction By Disclosure

OBJECTIVE: To facilitate the rapid breakdown of facades and norms against self-disclosure within a group.

PROCEDURE: Ask each participant to stand and share with the group a personal response to any one (or more, as the instructor desires) of these questions.

1. What is your greatest achievement?

2. What is your most prized possession?

3. If you could have a T-shirt printed with a message, what would it say?

4. What is the most fun that you ever had?

5. If you discovered that you had only one year to live, what would you do differently?

6. If you were stranded on a deserted island:

   a. What three books would you like to have along?
   b. What three people would you like to have there with you?

MATERIALS
REQUIRED: None.

APPROXIMATE
TIME
REQUIRED: One-half minute per person, per question.

SOURCE: R. Jones, ITT CBC, Rye, New York.

What's Your Image?

OBJECTIVE:
To become more aware of our public image, while also breaking the ice with other participants.

PROCEDURE:

1. Have each participant write four or five adjective words or phrases that describe his/her public image on a sheet of paper. Encourage them to be creative and disclose significant items of information.

2. Collect the sheets and mix them up.

3. Read the set of adjectives aloud to the group and have the group try to guess who is being described.

ALTERNATE
PROCEDURE:

1. Following step 2, distribute one sheet to each participant (not their own).

2. Have the participants mill around the room, seeking to identify the person described on their sheet.

DISCUSSION
QUESTIONS:

1. What did you learn about the ways in which people describe themselves?

2. What lessons in effective communication does this hold for us?

MATERIALS
REQUIRED:
Paper and pencils.

APPROXIMATE
TIME
REQUIRED:
Twenty-thirty minutes, depending on method chosen and the number of participants.

SOURCE:
Linda H. Harber, Virginia Commonwealth University, Richmond, Virginia.

Collecting Positive Strokes

OBJECTIVE: End a training program on a positive note.

PROCEDURE:

1. Provide each group member with a roster of names and one blank 3"x 5" card for each participant. At the beginning of the session, instruct them to observe their colleagues' behavior closely, and write one positive remark about each participant on a card. (The instructor may also choose to be a participant in this process--both as a contributor and as a participant.)

2. Toward the end of the program, collect the cards (be sure the intended recipient's name is on them), sort them into the appropriate envelopes and distribute them to each person. Allow adequate time to let each person scan quickly through their set. This allows each participant to leave the session with some positive feelings about themselves, even though the program may have been stressful.

ALTERNATIVE
PROCEDURE:

1. Ask them to provide each participant with "One tip for your success."

2. Ask them to complete this sentence for each participant, "I wish you would . . ."

DISCUSSION
QUESTIONS:

1. If time permits, ask each participant to read aloud the single card that made him or her feel the best.

2. Ask each participant to read aloud the single card that surprised (or confused) him or her.

MATERIALS
REQUIRED: One large envelope and one set of cards per participant.

APPROXIMATE
TIME
REQUIRED:

Assuming comments are recorded on a continuous basis, only ten minutes or so are required to collect the cards and, after sorting, distribute them.

SOURCE: Lee A. Beckner, Cameron Iron Works, Inc., Houston, Texas.

Concentric Circle Introductions

OBJECTIVES:

1. To break the ice at the beginning of a training program.

2. To help each participant meet several others.

PROCEDURE:

1. Prior to the session, identify eight to ten discussion topics that would give participants insight into one another and into the training program. For example, in a supervisory training program, the discussion topics might include: "Three things I like best about supervision;" "The person who gives me the most trouble at work and how I deal with that person;" "I'm attending this session . . .;" and so forth.

2. Have participants form two concentric circles in which each person in the inner circle faces one person in the outer circle to form pairs, as shown on the following page. (If the number of participants is odd, either form one group into a trio or join one of the circles yourself.)

3. Have the pairs exchange names and discuss one of the pre-planned questions for three minutes.

4. After three minutes have passed, ring a cowbell or blow a whistle to get participants' attention--the noise level is likely to be quite high if you are working with more than a few participants. Then ask people in the outer circle to move several steps to the right to form new pairs.

5. Repeat steps 3 and 4 with another question until the group's energy begins to decline, or time runs out.

DISCUSSION QUESTIONS:

1. What tentative opinions have you formed about the other participants in this program?

2. What ideas do you want to discuss further with other participants?

MATERIALS REQUIRED:

Cowbell, whistle or other noisemaker; pre-planned questions.

APPROXIMATE TIME REQUIRED:

Variable, depending on the number of repetitions.

SOURCE:

Dr. Ed Kur, Arizona State University, Tempe, Arizona.

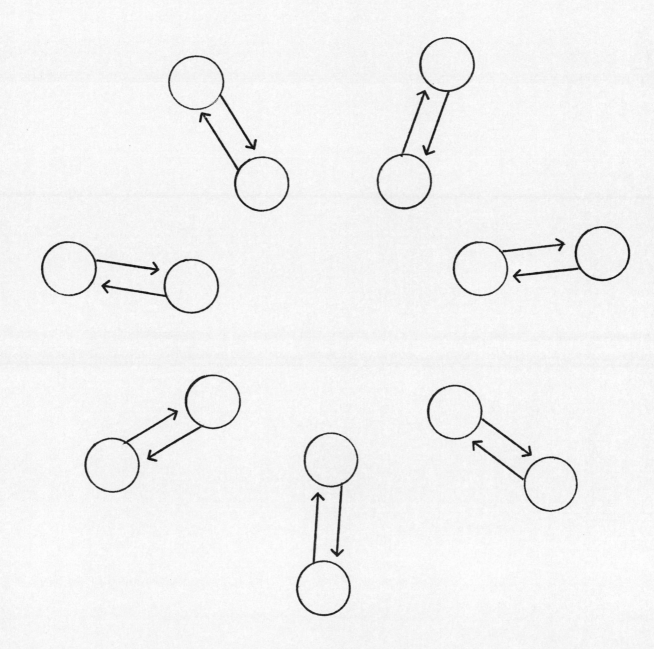

Solving Ant-i-grams

OBJECTIVE: To break the ice among participants, or to facilitate trainee return from coffee breaks by catching their attention.

PROCEDURE: Prepare a set of cartoons (ant-i-grams), each of which depicts a word or phrase that involves the word "ant" somewhere within it. Display one of these just before each coffee break and ask the group members to guess at the real word.

Examples include:

1. Antarctic (an ant shivering at the North Pole)

2. Antiaircraft (an ant riding atop a plane)

3. Antelope (a boy and girl ant climbing down a ladder to get married)

4. Square Dance (ants^2)

5. Anticlimax (an ant climbing up an axe).

6. Others -- Use your imagination!

MATERIALS
REQUIRED: Transparencies, or freehand drawings on a flip chart or chalkboard.

APPROXIMATE
TIME
REQUIRED: One-three minutes each.

SOURCE: Hugh Braun, Gateway Technical Institute, Kenosha, Wisconsin.

1.

NORTH POLE

2.

3.

2

4.

5.

Performance Appraisal

OBJECTIVES: To be used as a "tongue in cheek" handout in assessing or analyzing performance; to humorously illustrate the different kinds of people in an organization.

PROCEDURE: May be used as a comic relief at the end of an arduous session, or at any time when a break from routine is deemed helpful. Distribute copies of the form on the following page to participants. No comment is required but some categories may bring forth discussion of participants.

MATERIALS
REQUIRED: Handout sheet.

APPROXIMATE
TIME
REQUIRED: Five minutes.

SOURCE: Unknown.

GUIDE TO EVALUATION OF PERSONNEL

PERFORMANCE DEGREES

PERFORMANCE FACTORS	FAR EXCEEDS JOB REQUIREMENTS	EXCEEDS JOB REQUIREMENTS	MEETS JOB REQUIREMENTS	NEEDS SOME IMPROVEMENT	DOES NOT MEET MINIMUM REQUIREMENTS
QUALITY	LEAPS TALL BUILDINGS WITH A SINGLE BOUND	MUST TAKE A RUNNING START TO LEAP OVER TALL BUILD-INGS	CAN ONLY LEAP OVER A SHORT BUILDING WITH NO SPIRES	CRASHES INTO BUILDING WHEN ATTEMPTING TO JUMP OVER THEM	CANNOT RECOG-NIZE BUILDINGS AT ALL--WHAT'S MORE JUMP
TIMELINESS	IS FASTER THAN A SPEEDING BULLET	IS AS FAST AS A SPEEDING BULLET	NOT QUITE AS FAST AS A SPEEDING BULLET	WOULD YOU BE-LIEVE A SLOW BULLET	WOUNDS SELF WITH BULLET WHEN ATTEMPT-ING TO SHOOT GUN
INITIATIVE	IS STRONGER THAN A LOCO-MOTIVE	IS STRONGER THAN A BULL ELEPHANT	IS STRONGER THAN A BULL	SHOOTS THE BULL	SMELLS LIKE A BULL
ADAPTABILITY	WALKS ON WATER CONSISTENTLY	WALKS ON WATER IN EMERGENCIES	WASHES WITH WATER	DRINKS WATER	PASSES WATER IN EMERGENCIES
COMMUNICATION	TALKS WITH GOD	TALKS WITH THE ANGELS	TALKS TO HIM-SELF	ARGUES WITH HIMSELF	LOSES THOSE ARGUMENTS

263

XI.

TRANSFER

OF

TRAINING

My Contract With Myself

OBJECTIVE: To facilitate transfer of training to the job.

PROCEDURE: After each module, block or unit of instruction,
                      have the participants prepare a contract with
                      themselves as shown on the next page.

                      At the conclusion of the workshop or seminar,
                      participants may:

                      1. Review and update each module, block or
                          unit contract;

                      2. Consolidate all previous contracts into
                          one final contract;

                      3. Use the contracts to prepare a "Letter to
                          Myself" (Games Trainers Play by Newstrom
                          and Scannell, McGraw-Hill Book Company,
                          1980, p. 301.)

MATERIALS
REQUIRED: Preprinted form on following page.

APPROXIMATE
TIME
REQUIRED: Three-five minutes at the end of each module and
                      five-ten minutes at the end of the workshop or
                      seminar.

SOURCE: Gail D. O'Byrne, Basics of Supervision Workshop,
                      State of Washington.

MY CONTRACT WITH MYSELF

My key learning for this section *(task/activity)*

In my current position, I can use this
    information to

I am going to share this information with

I plan to develop my skills in this area by

Videotape Playback

OBJECTIVE: To "replay" previous training sessions attended and to summarize key points that were covered.

PROCEDURE: At the end of the training session (preferably one that covered several topics), ask the group to simulate viewing a videotape recording of all the sessions they are just completing. As they "view" the tapes, suggest they especially "tune" in a particular session or segment that had special meaning--or triggered a novel idea for application for their jobs.

Allow two-three minutes for individual time and ask group to form subgroups of three-four members to discuss their main points. Ask a spokesperson in each group to identify that respective group's best idea.

DISCUSSION
QUESTIONS:

1. Why did you select the particular segment or idea that you did?

2. When others reported, did you have the same recollections or reactions as they? Why? Why not?

3. Were there some portions you completely forgot about? Why do you suppose this happens?

MATERIALS
REQUIRED: None.

APPROXIMATE
TIME
REQUIRED: Fifteen minutes.

SOURCE: Unknown.

Support Groups

OBJECTIVE:
To increase the probability that newly-learned concepts and skills will be applied, by creating a network of relationships to provide greater psychological support and reinforcement.

PROCEDURE:
At the end of a training module or session, provide trainees with a diagram like the one on the following page. Have them record their name in the center circle. Direct them to think of other members of the training group whom they could help, assist, or support. The assistance may be technical or emotional, short-term or long, social or work-related. Have them record the names of the persons they are willing to HELP in the top row of circles.

Then request that they consider the persons they feel that they could most benefit from. These persons might be open, sharing, interested, skilled, comfortable, stimulating, etc. Have them record the names of the persons they would like to draw help from in the bottom row of circles. Provide a mechanism (e.g., registrant roster) whereby addresses and phone numbers can be readily obtained.

If time permits, allow the class members to circulate, expressing their respective offers and requests to other persons. Encourage them to follow through at an early date by visiting, phoning, or writing their support people.

DISCUSSION QUESTIONS:
1. Did you have trouble identifying five persons in each category? If so, why?

2. How much overlap was there between those you wanted to help and their perception of you as a potential helper?

3. What strategies do you have for helping others? For seeking help from others?

MATERIALS REQUIRED:
Handout.

APPROXIMATE TIME REQUIRED:
Ten minutes (longer if they circulate).

SOURCE:
Adapted from Tom Ferguson, "Your Support Group", MEDICAL SELF-CARE, 7, Winter, 1979-80, p. 9.

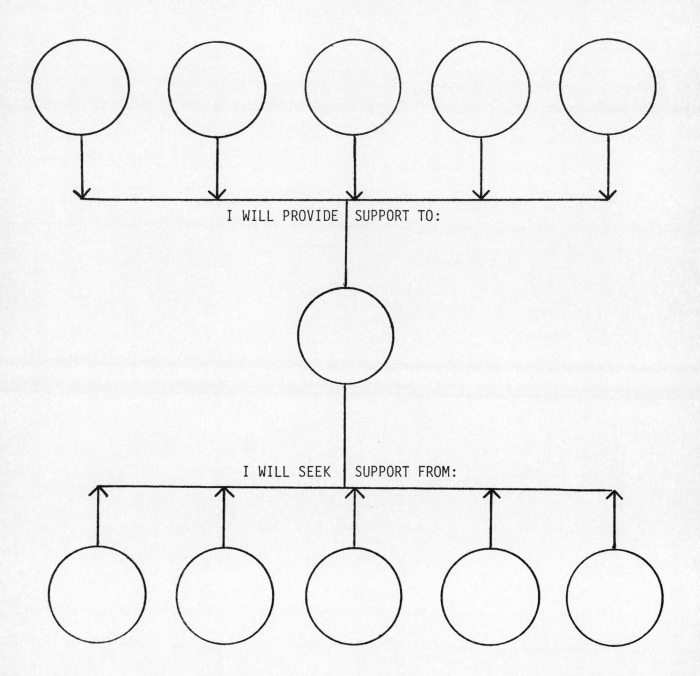

I WILL PROVIDE | SUPPORT TO:

I WILL SEEK | SUPPORT FROM:

275

Solving Rubik's Cube

OBJECTIVE: To provide a dramatic visual model to stimulate retention of important concepts in supervisory development.

PROCEDURE: Display one of the six-colored cubes to the participants in an introductory management seminar. Inquire how many of them

1. Have one in their house;

2. Have played with it; and

3. Have solved it.

(Note: The answers to 1 and 2 will be relatively high, while the response to the third question will be relatively low.)

Then ask them to brainstorm all the major descriptive phrases that characterize the process of solving Rubik's cube when it is in disarray. Record these brief descriptors visibly in front of them as they are offered. (A sample list of such items follows this exercise. It could also be used for visual presentational purposes, if time pressures are great.)

Now suggest to them that you believe that Rubik's cube represents a close and powerful analog to the process of being a first-line supervisor. Quick review of the list generated should show the face validity of this conclusion. Then conclude by encouraging them to keep Rubik's cube in mind as they participate in various modules of the seminar and particularly back on their jobs.

ALTERNATE
PROCEDURES:

1. Substitute other groups for supervisor (e.g., salespersons, trainers, tellers) and the exercise works equally well.

2. An effective reinforcer is to give each participant their own Rubik's cube (or at least a color picture of one) at the end of the seminar.

DISCUSSION
QUESTIONS:

1. What is the most challenging part of your job?

2. What resources are available to help you improve your skills?

3. What are the common reasons why (new) supervisors fail?

```
MATERIALS
REQUIRED:              One cube and a flip chart.

APPROXIMATE
TIME
REQUIRED:              Fifteen minutes.

SOURCE:                Unknown.
```

CHARACTERISTICS: FRUSTRATING

CHALLENGING

REWARDING (IF EVEN PARTIAL SUCCESS IS ACHIEVED)

LARGE NUMBER OF ALTERNATIVE POSSIBILITIES EXIST

A SOLUTION DOES EXIST

ONE ERROR CAN INVALIDATE EARLIER EFFORTS

TIME CONSUMING

SOME KNOWLEDGE OR TRAINING IS HIGHLY DESIRABLE

DEMONSTRATION BY ANOTHER HELPS GREATLY

PRACTICE IS REQUIRED TO ACHIEVE PROFICIENCY.

The Pocket Card

OBJECTIVE: To provide a frequent mental/physical stimulus to remind trainees of the need to practice a new behavior.

PROCEDURE: At the end of a training module or session, ask the trainees these three questions:

1. What are the three things that you intend to do differently (or wish to accomplish) in the next month as a product of this program?

2. Would you be more likely to do those things if you were reminded of them frequently?

3. How often do you reach into your pocket or purse on a daily basis?

Distribute the printed cards, with space provided for the trainees to describe their three goals. After they have filled in their cards, instruct them to carry the plastic-enclosed card with them at all times and mentally review the goals and their progress toward them each time their hands (or eyes) contact the card.

DISCUSSION QUESTIONS:

1. What are some of the goals that you chose?

2. What actions of yours are necessary to accomplish those goals?

3. What cooperation from others (or what material) is required to help you be successful?

4. What problems are you likely to encounter? How can these be prevented/reduced/overcome?

MATERIALS REQUIRED: Printed wallet-sized cards; plastic enclosures.

APPROXIMATE TIME REQUIRED: Five minutes.

SOURCE: Joel Weldon & Associates, Scottsdale, Arizona.

Red, White, And Blue Chips

OBJECTIVE: To impress upon participants the importance of setting and following priorities.

PROCEDURE:

1. Obtain a large quantity of red, white, and blue poker chips. There should be mostly white ones and least blue ones.

2. Arrange them in three piles on a table in front of the training room.

3. Ask for two volunteers. Instruct them that their objective is to obtain the greatest total value of chips that they can pick up in a thirty-second period of time. Count the number of each color chips that they obtain.

4. Ask for two more volunteers. Instruct them that the blue chips are worth $25, the red chips worth $4, and the white chips worth $1 each. Give them the same objective and time period and count the number of each color chips that they obtain.

DISCUSSION
QUESTIONS:

1. In managing our time/energy, how does it help to know the relative value (payoff) of the activities that we are engaging in?

2. In managing our time/energy, how does it help to prioritize our activities by spending our time on the most-important-first items?

3. How does this exercise relate to what you will do on the job tomorrow?

MATERIALS
REQUIRED: A large supply of chips in three colors.

APPROXIMATE
TIME
REQUIRED: Ten minutes.

SOURCE: Susan Colby, Target Stores, Minneapolis, Minnesota.

Test Your Constraints

OBJECTIVE: To stimulate participants to identify, classify, and mentally test which factors are most significant in keeping them from starting or stopping something.

PROCEDURE: 1. Explain that people are often boxed in by various constraints. However, it is our perception of these limitations that creates the most significant barriers, and these need to be explored.

2. Ask each participant to think of something that he or she would either like to start doing or stop doing.

3. Tell them to list all the things that now prevent them from accomplishing their objective. Then have them categorize them as:

   a. Realistic and rigid (e.g., upper management edicts).

   b. Moderately firm (e.g., standard policies and practices that are usually inviolable).

   c. Flexible (implicit procedures or interpersonal/ intergroup relations).

   d. Illusionary (partly based on facts but largely embellished by our imagination).

4. Point out that one organization (General Electric) discovered that over 95% of the constraints identified by its foremen and first-line supervisors were classified as either flexible or illusionary.

5. Encourage them to test their limits--be willing to experiment--take a risk and see what happens.

DISCUSSION
QUESTIONS: 1. What kinds of things did you identify as something you would like to start or stop doing?

2. What were some of the illusionary constraints that you identified?

3. Give an example of an action plan for overcoming one of the constraints.

MATERIALS
REQUIRED: None.

APPROXIMATE
TIME
REQUIRED: From thirty minutes to three hours, depending on the amount of group discussion and degree of workshop orientation that you wish to take.

SOURCE: Richard D. Colvin, General Electric Management Development
                 Institute, as described in "Increasing Personal Effective-
                 ness", TRAINING AND DEVELOPMENT JOURNAL, January 1978,
                 pp. 30-33.

XII.

TEAM BUILDING

Team Building

OBJECTIVE:

To allow participants to "blue-sky" or fantasize their ideal training program.

PROCEDURE:

Divide the group into subsets of four-five persons each. Tell them they have just received a call from their VP, Human Resource Development (or similar authority) that the organization has just allocated $_____ (an extremely high figure is suggested, i.e., $300,000) to be used strictly as you identify. Let the group write down their "wish list" individually with some approximate budget figure for each item. (An example could be to visit personally five of the top Human Resource Development authorities in the world. Cost would include airfare, food, lodging, consulting fees, etc.)

Following five-ten minutes of individual ideation, each group discusses the individual priority listings and attempts consensus on a group list. Group records and reports their results to entire audience.

DISCUSSION
QUESTIONS:

1. After you had written your individual "wish list", how many of you greatly altered your ideas or budgets?

2. While "group think" collective ideation ordinarily produces a better result, are there some cautions as well?

3. If your top priority is really important, what are some ways we can convince our boss to budget the necessary dollars?

MATERIALS
REQUIRED:

Paper, flip chart.

APPROXIMATE
TIME
REQUIRED:

Thirty-forty minutes.

SOURCE:

Varied.

Team Charades

OBJECTIVE: To establish quickly cohesiveness in new teams that must work together in a training situation for the remainder of the day or course.

PROCEDURE:

1. Divide the participants into teams, based upon either personal preference or some previously established criteria or method.

2. Ask each group to choose a name for their team that will identify it for the duration of the session.

3. Call upon each group to act out its name in "charades" fashion, while other groups try to guess the name of the group on stage.

MATERIALS
REQUIRED: None.

APPROXIMATE
TIME
REQUIRED: Fifteen minutes (depends on number of groups and the ease with which group names are guessed).

SOURCE: Robert A. Vannerson, Liberty Mutual Insurance Company, Boston, Massachusetts.

Bests And Worsts

OBJECTIVE: To introduce complex topics in an enjoyable way.

PROCEDURE:

1. Ask participants to yell out the best and worst examples of the topic. For instance, in a train-the-trainer program ask participants to identify the best and worst characteristics of public speakers they know. Write the two lists on newsprint, chalkboard or screen.

2. For each item on each list ask participants to share reasons for placing that item on their list.

3. After discussing each item, have participants work in buzz groups to answer the discussion questions below.

4. Have each buzz group report answers to the total group and discuss.

DISCUSSION QUESTIONS:

1. Form a list of seven "Do's" based on our discussion of the "Best" list.

2. Form a list of seven "Don'ts" based on our discussion of the "Worst" list.

3. Alternatively: Based on our discussion of the two lists, what topics do you believe we should specifically address in this training program?

MATERIALS REQUIRED:

Newsprint, chalkboard or screen and projector.

APPROXIMATE TIME REQUIRED:

Twenty minutes.

SOURCE:

Ed Kur, Arizona State University, Tempe, Arizona.

What's The Problem?

OBJECTIVE:

To encourage participants to identify objectives and problems for a given topic and build the agenda on those specified areas.

PROCEDURE:

Mention that too many training sessions or meetings may miss the mark because participants never know the expected outcomes or really "buy" into the trainer's objectives. To prevent that from happening, explain that you're going to give everyone a chance to help clarify the objectives for this session and then help in suggesting concrete ideas to achieve these goals.

Set the stage by introducing the scheduled session or meeting topic, e.g., "Our goal this morning is to identify at least a dozen ways we can secure new accounts..." Make certain all attendees have enough background information or experience on the assigned topics.

Ask participants to think about the problem or topic for a few minutes and then give them eight-ten additional minutes for jotting down the major obstacles they can identify that might preclude our reaching the goal.

Form groups of four-five and get consensus on their top five concerns. Ask each group recorder to write these on flip chart paper. After all reports are made, the listed problems become the agenda, and the balance of the time is spent working on these.

An optional approach is to assign one or a series of the listed problems back to the groups and discuss for 30-40 minutes. Reporters then bring their proposed solutions to the entire group.

MATERIALS
REQUIRED:

Flip chart.

APPROXIMATE
TIME
REQUIRED:

Forty-sixty minutes.

SOURCE:

Unknown.

Department X-Y-Z

OBJECTIVE:
To build a spirit of teamwork in groups and to practice creativity and informal platform skills.

PROCEDURE:
Break group into subgroups of five people. Each subset is assigned to a "new" department or agency within the company, organization, etc. The team leader is given a card with a nonsensical acronym (3-4 letters) printed on it. The team then decides what the letters stand for and describes to the group the name of the "department" and what its mission and objectives are. An example could be PHDS. The team might create "Productivity and Human Design Systems" and then go on and report the kind of activities and scope of this mythical department. (Allow 8-10 minutes for brainstorming and 3-4 minutes for each team report.) A panel could be named to select the winning team.

MATERIALS
REQUIRED:
3" x 5" cards.

APPROXIMATE
TIME
REQUIRED:
Twenty-thirty minutes dependent on size of group.

SOURCE:
Dr. Robert Kreitner, Arizona State University, Tempe, Arizona.

"Help Wanted"

In a continuing effort to share the hundreds of exercises, activities and games used by trainers, we'd like to solicit your assistance. If you've developed an original activity, or have used one that might be shared with fellow trainers, we'd appreciate hearing about it.

You can use this form (make copies if needed) and send it in. If you can help identify the source or originator, we can research it from that point. THANK YOU.

TITLE: _____

OBJECTIVE: _____

_____

PROCEDURE: _____

_____

_____

_____

_____

_____

_____

_____

_____

_____

_____

MATERIALS
REQUIRED: _____

APPROXIMATE
TIME REQUIRED: _____

SOURCE: _____

Please return to: Edward E. Scannell, Director, University Conference Bureau, Arizona State University, Tempe, Arizona 85287 or John Newstrom, School of Business & Economics 110, University of Minnesota-Duluth, Duluth, Minnesota 55812.

About The Authors

EDWARD E. SCANNELL
The Director of the University Conference Bureau at Arizona State University, Edward E. Scannell has previously taught in the College of Business Administration at A.S.U. and the University of Northern Iowa.

He has been on the National Board of Directors of the American Society for Training and Development since 1974 and was elected ASTD National President in 1982.

A member of the National Speakers Association, he has given over 2,000 presentations to local, state, regional and national meetings. Active also in civic and professional associations, he serves on the Board of several other organizations, including the Tempe Chamber of Commerce, Meeting Planners International (Sunbelt Chapter) and the Arizona Business, Industry, Education Council.

Scannell has written and co-authored six other books and over 25 articles in the field of Human Resource Development. He is listed in several directories, including Who's Who In The West, Men of Achievement, and Dictionary of International Biography.

JOHN W. NEWSTROM
Dr. Newstrom is Professor of Management and Industrial Relations at the University of Minnesota-Duluth, and served as Head of the Business Administration Department at the University.

His primary interests lie in the areas of management development, participative management, and alternative work schedules. He is co-author of three other books, including Organizational Behavior: Readings and Exercises (with Keith Davis). He has served on the editorial review boards for the Academy of Management Review, The Personnel Administrator, and the Journal of Management Development.

A ten-year member of ASTD, past president of the Valley of the Sun Chapter, and now a member of the

Lake Superior Chapter, he has co-presented several sessions at National ASTD Conferences, and is the team leader for ASTD's "The Training Function". He has published numerous articles in the Training and Development Journal on such topics as evaluation, needs analysis, methods, and transfer of training. His chapter on Employee Training and Development appears in the Encyclopedia of Professional Management. He is also the co-author of the popular book, Games Trainers Play, McGraw-Hill (with Edward E. Scannell).